To Robin,

# Grace Notes

with laughter +
prayers —

Brian Doyle

To Ethel Clancey Doyle,
who loves with all her might,
to Cynthia Shoshana Ozick,
with prayers and gratitude,
and in memory of my friend
Becky Houck, 1950-2009

# Grace Notes

true stories about sins, sons, shrines,
silence, marriage, homework, jail, miracles, dads,
legs, basketball, the sinewy grace of women,
bullets, music, infirmaries, the power of powerlessness,
the ubiquity of prayers, & some other matters

BRIAN DOYLE

**GRACE NOTES**
by Brian Doyle

Edited by Gregory F. Augustine Pierce
Cover design by Tom A. Wright
Cover photo, "Argentine Tree Frog," by James Balog, jamesbalog.com
Interior drawings by Mary Miller Doyle
Text design and typesetting by Patricia A. Lynch

Versions of these articles were published previously. See "Provenance" at the end of the book.

Published by ACTA Publications, 4848 N. Clark Street, Chicago, IL 60640, (800) 397-2282, www.actapublications.com

Library of Congress Catalog number: 2011927342
ISBN: 978-0-87946-434-9
Printed in the United States of America by McNaughton and Gunn
Year 20 19 18 17 16 15 14 13 12 11
Printing 15 14 13 12 11 10 9 8 7 6 5 4 3 2 First

# CONTENTS

# III.

# FOREWORD HO

The good sweet Lord alone knows why a book of stories by one muddled guy would demand an introductory note *by the same muddled guy*, but it seems to me that a team meeting, as it were, before we get started is a good idea. The pieces of writing in the pages that follow are animated by some people and remarks that to me are compass points, lodestars, maps to steer by.

*Attentiveness is the beginning of all prayer*, says the great poet Mary Oliver, and *everything that lives is holy*, says the confusing poet Billy Blake, and *all the way to heaven is heaven*, says the tart Saint Catherine of Siena, and *let grief be a falling leaf*, says the testy poet Van Morrison, and *grace under duress is the great story of us*, says the undersigned muddleness. How we reach for each other and listen to each other's music and share stories like the most amazing and nutritious food – that's what we are all here for.

Me personally I think stories are the coolest wildest prayers there are. It's no accident that the skinny Jewish guy who wandered around Judea some years ago was a terrific storyteller, his tales mysterious and shimmering, wriggling their way through the centuries even unto our day, and now into the ears and hearts of our children and our children's children; stories matter, stories live forever, stories are how we shuffle quickest toward the Mercy greater than the ocean and denser than the stars in the sky. Stories maybe save lives. They sure saved mine.

*Brian Doyle*
*Portland, Oregon*

# PROLOGUE

# The Genius of American Catholicism

All of the stories in this slim frog-faced volume are, in the end, about praying, in wild ways, and attentiveness, which is prayer, and the usually confusing and mysterious and sometimes very painful gift of What Is, which is the coolest gift imaginable, and you only receive it once, as far as I can tell. A lot of these stories, in short, are about spiritual matters, and a lot of them also use that most riveting religion Catholicism as a prism, a way of being, an approach, a diving board, so maybe we should start this book by having a chat about the brilliance of Catholicism, which endures beneath the greed and violence and rapacious nature of the religion as practiced. Beneath the religion is something of genius, and we never talk much about that. So let's do so for a moment.

---

Let's focus on the genius of Catholicism, which is the fact that it is illogical, unreasonable, unthinkable, unprovable, nonsensical, counter-cultural, and in direct defiance of all evidence and human history. Isn't that great? Isn't the loopiness at the center of it the best thing of all? We never admit that — but maybe we should celebrate it. Could it be that the wildness of it is the ring of truth? Let me get this straight: the very essence of our common belief, the polestar by which we steer our lives, is the fact that a thin young Jewish man two thousand years ago insisted that life defeats death, hope defeats despair, light defeats darkness? That's ridiculous. That's silly. The evidence is everywhere against it. But he insisted on it, to the point of death — and whether you believe he rose from the dead and again walked the earth for three days, asking for something to eat, or you do not believe such a tall tale, the inarguable fact is that his insistence, his story, his wild message, has persisted and grown and permutated beyond comprehension. Why? It's not only the religious structure built atop his message that helped his voice persist into our time — I believe it is his sheer insistence on that which is wholly unreasonable that touches us deepest in our hearts, that reaches down and makes us shiver in our deepest bones, that rings the very deep bell of truth inside us. I believe his message and his genius has persisted because it is finally about hope and about the very deepest feelings we have as human animals — feelings so deep inside us that they burst out only occasionally, and are often terrifying and rattling when they erupt. Because hope flies in the face of every shred of evidence, I believe in it. Isn't that wonderful? Isn't belief that hope defeats despair a wild leap like the ones we take when we commit to marriage, to a vocation, to a tumultuous democracy? Isn't hope a quiet grin like the one on the frog on the cover? Isn't it foolish to believe in light and life, given all the evidence against? But doesn't being foolish often feel altogether right, in every cell of your body? Wouldn't a testy insistence on believing only that which you can see and touch and smell seem finally like a defeat, a retreat, a surrender, a loneliness?

———

Let's focus on the Americanness of American Catholicism — the odd sweet mix of thorny prickly independence and warm brave thorough communal fabric that is this country. Let's look at Catholicism for a moment through the American lens, and see what happened to it here, on what many of the first people here called Turtle Island, on this rich new continent, in this utterly unique national idea — what happened to an ancient religion when it became the blood and breath and song and hope of people here? Maybe American Catholics like

Flannery O'Connor and Andre Dubus and Joseph Bernadin, all of whom were respectful of the past but looking past and through it — maybe they are dreamers of the future reality — as Christ and Gandhi and Tutu were and are dreamers of the substance of things hoped for. For many years Catholicism simply fought for its life in this land, fought to exist, fought not to be crushed. But now that we are established, now that there are sixty million American Catholics and more coming every day, now that Catholic colleges and universities have become more and more the factories that produce generations of eager, curious, selfless young Catholics and have risen ever higher in national prominence and voice, now that Catholic artists like Alice McDermott and Bruce Springsteen have been acclaimed among the best in American history — now what? Might the story of American Catholicism now be less insisting on the rights of Catholic Americans than insisting on the heights of American Catholics? What now will we be? How can we elevate and energize and shove and rebuild and resurrect the Catholic idea here? We American Catholics are of the old church, of the Old World, as we are of Judaism, of the rootstock, but in both cases we have forged on ahead. The old battles are fought and won, and we are free to go...where? Could it be that American Catholics, having been seared with fury over rape, denial, and lies about rapists among us, will emerge from the ash to shape the energy of the young into a faith that carries hope and healing into millions more hearts? That finds ways to heal rifts among the Christian tribes? That finds brotherhood with Islam, which also bows to the One and to the Madonna? The faith we were raised in has passed — what is the faith in which our children will raise theirs?

———

Let's think for a bit not of Catholicism the religion, but of Catholicism the genius idea — an idea that has everything to do with relentless unquenchable irresistible crazy insistent hope. It may be that the human capacity to hope, to dream what might be, to have visions, is finally the reason we are here, the reason we evolved to this point, and our greatest responsibility as creatures of the Lord. Some questions, then, for us to chew on: Could it be that our greatest talent and tool and skill is the ability to insist on the illogical and unreasonable, and so force the holy peace of the future into being? Could we be the means by which the future will be born? Could the Christ in us be the greatest evolutionary tool of all? Could our deep crazy insistence that everything is miraculous and soaked in holiness be the very means by which human beings finally achieve what the Creator hoped against all evidence that we might achieve? Could our utterly unreasonable faith that human beings can rise to astonishing grace and courage and creativity be the very reason that we are given free will with which to crash or soar? Could our genius for hope be the only tool that in the end defeats suffering? Could our absolute conviction that the thin Jewish man long ago was right when he insisted that hope defeats despair, life defeats death, light defeats darkness be the road that carries all of humanity past its addiction to violence? Could the secret be not Resurrection of one man, but Resurrection of a whole species, as it were? Could the secret to a world of peace and laughter be not Christ, but Christ in us? Could Christ-in-us be a far vaster idea and gift than merely for Christians? Could Christ-in-us be the secret to all real religions? Could Christ-in-us be the reason human beings were lifted above the other species of living beings, and given the gifts of sadness and reflection, mysticism and vision, brains with unplumbed depths? Could Christ-in-us, the divine splinter slammed into every heart, be what we are here for? Could that be why his story is so persistent and insistent and mysterious and uneasy? Could his story be far bigger than the religion we built on it, bigger than any religion?

So much of religion is mere cultural drape and accident — but spirituality is pan-cultural. We are all haunted spiritual beings struggling for words to clothe the unimaginable but undeniable. We all know full well deep in our hearts that which is holy and that which is evil. We know what is love and what is sham. We know that religions are only languages and vocabularies and symbol systems for us to use as grappling hooks — they are lovely languages, and no one loves the redolent mythic brilliant magic and ritual and succor of Catholicism more than me. But it is a small house in a universe of mansions. *There are many mansions in my Father's house....* Yet it seems to me that Catholicism, and especially American Catholicism, catches at more of the deep human spiritual genius than any other faith. Judaism and Islam are finally abject worship of the all-powerful One, and brilliantly designed systems for living in a tumultuous world where all are weak; Hinduism seems to me a dense lovely ancient seething grappling with all the energies and forces of the world, a wondrously tendrilled attempt to name them, put faces to them, ascribe them powers, make of them entities to entreat; Buddhism, though closest to Catholicism in its insistence that attentiveness is the door to holiness, is also a panoply of sacred energies and powers; but Catholicism seems far more joyous, far more celebratory, far more invitation to partnership, far more expectation of responsibility in creating the wonder of the future than mere acceptance of Mastery. We worship the One, from whom all things come, but we savor the genius of the Son, who is us. That is the point. That is the brilliance. That is the genius. It isn't that he rose — it's that he rises again and again and again and again day after day city after city soul after soul. Catholicism is not Master and Servant — it is Father asking children to rise to their best selves, to accept responsibility, to use their holy tools to create what can be. In a real sense we as nominal adults are merely hoary older teenagers, with all the glorious energy and creativity and possibility of a teen, as well as all the selfishness and blindness and self-absorption and laziness and disorganization. All is not ordained — from the tools we have been given, the incredible one-in-ten-billion-years tools each of us is given — we are asked to help create. We are asked to be Artists! What a gift! What a joy! What an astonishing and terrifying assignment!

—•—

And deep deep deep down in the bones of Catholicism there is a wisdom beyond words. You know and I know there is so much more going on than ever we could see, could sense, could identify, could struggle to name. We know there are worlds beyond worlds; this is the great energy of our sciences, that we discover and discover and we never come to the end of it; if we think this to be true of the universe itself, can we think it is not true of all aspects of the universe? And again we struggle for words to describe what we know to be true but cannot articulate — visions and hallucinations, voices and signs, interventions and miracles.... It is unreasonable to believe, illogical, nonsensical — but it seems to me impossible not to believe. To believe only in your senses — is that selfish? Is it a function of fear? Is the intellect the only door? It comes down to hope. That is the food of this nation and this religion. That is the great song of the human being. It doesn't make sense. But again and again we do not make sense in every conceivable arena and again and again we punch through sense and reason and logic into the far, far deeper ocean for which the only word that applies is love — a love nearly beyond our ken — but not quite. The genius of Catholicism is that Christ is us — inside each of us is the extraordinary key to the substance of things hoped for. The genius of Americanness is independence married to responsibility. Here we are free to reach for the stars, to create anything we can dream, to hold hands with our fellows and leap for the light. I think here Catholicism may surge forward into a new rich wild creativity that opens yet another door toward who we might finally be—if we drop our weapons, and remove the beams from our eyes, and mill our extraordinary gifts into the fabric of a world where no child weeps, no child is terrified, wars are a memory, and we eat wonder all day like the most amazing and nutritious food. It can happen, you know, and if it happens I think it may happen here. There was never a national idea like America, and for all the violence and greed of our history there is still no idea as brave and wild and nonsensical and brilliant and generous as America. There was never an idea like Catholicism, and for all the violence and greed of that far longer story, there is still no idea as brave and wild and unreasonable and generous at its heart. What if the wildest national idea and the wildest religious idea kept going and growing and influencing each other and sending out new brilliant agents of hope into the future? What might happen then? Now that America and Catholicism are married, what will be their sweet wild child?

# I.

# A SIN

Committed a sin yesterday, in the hallway, at noon. I roared at my son, I grabbed him by the shirt collar, I frightened him so badly that he cowered and wept, and when he turned to run I grabbed him by the arm so roughly that he flinched, and it was that flicker of fear and pain across his face, the bright eager holy riveting face I have loved for ten years, that stopped me then and haunts me this morning; for I am the father of his fear, I sent it snarling into his heart, and I can never get it out now, which torments me.

Yes, he was picking on his brother, and yes, he had picked on his brother all morning, and yes, this was the culmination of many edgy incidents already, and no, he hadn't paid the slightest attention to warnings and remonstrations and fulminations, and yes, he had been snide and supercilious all day, and yes, he had deliberately done exactly the thing he had specifically been warned not to do, for murky reasons; but still, I roared at him and grabbed him and terrified him and made him cower, and now there is a dark evil wriggle between us that makes me sit here with my hands over my face, ashamed to the bottom of my bones.

I do not know how sins can be forgiven. I grasp the concept, I admire the genius of the idea, I suspect it to be the seed of all real peace, I savor the Tutus and Gandhis who have had the mad courage to live by it, but I do not understand how foul can be made fair. What is done cannot be undone, and my moment of rage in the hallway is an indelible scar on my son's heart and mine, and while my heart is a ragged old bag after nearly half a century of slings and stings, his is still new, eager, open, suggestible, innocent; he has committed only the small sins of a child, the halting first lies, the failed test paper hidden in the closet, the window broken in petulance, the stolen candy bar, the silent witness as a classmate is bullied, the insults flung like bitter knives.

Whereas I am a man, and have had many lies squirming in my mouth, and have committed calumny, and far too often evaded the mad ragged Christ, ignored his stink, his rotten teeth, his cloak of soggy newspapers, his voice of broken glass.

No God can forgive what we do to each other; only the injured can summon that extraordinary grace; and where such grace is born we cannot say, for all our fitful genius and miraculous machinery. We use the word *God* so easily, so casually, as if our label for the incomprehensible meant anything at all; and we forget all too easily that the wriggle of holy is born only through the stammer and stumble of us, who are always children. So we turn again and again to one another, and bow, and ask forgiveness, and mill what mercy we can muster from the muddle of our hearts.

The instant I let go of my son's sinewy arm in the hallway he sprinted away and slammed the door and flew off the porch and ran down the street and I stood there simmering in shame. Then I walked down the hill into the laurel thicket as dense and silent as the dawn of the world and found him there huddled and sobbing. We knelt in the moist green dark for a long time, not saying anything, the branches burly and patient. Finally I asked quietly for his forgiveness and he asked for mine and we walked out of the woods hand in hand, changed men.

# ADVICE TO MY SON

Don't *eat* that. Do ask questions. Do not use that tone of voice with me, young man. Do pick up the wet towel from the floor and hang it either on the closet door or on the back of your bedroom door or in the bathroom as you have been asked to do since the beginning of recorded history. Do not play my old records at 78 revolutions per minute and sing along like you are a squirrel on major recreational medicine. Do ask the girl out even if you are absolutely sure she will say no and your friends will berate you and her friends will point you out in the hallway and whisper the words *doofus* and *geek*. Do not do your math homework on the bus early in the morning when you know and I know that you have a history test first period and a science test second period and you have technically actually studied for neither of these rigorous intellectual challenges. Do pick up your own plate after dinner and rinse it in the sink and contemplate the remote possibility of actually picking up any other single dish or plate on the table and bringing it all the way in from the dining room to the kitchen which is as you know a yawning chasm of about seven feet. Do not keep answering a question with a question in a clear and deliberate effort to drive your mother into a frenzy awesome in its implications because if your mother loses her quick and supple mind we will all be in the poorhouse peeling mice for a living. Do write your thank-you notes to aunts uncles grandparents and friends of the family who have showered you with more cash for your birthday than your father has ever in his whole life had on his person or indeed except in miraculous moments in the bank. Do not bump, strike, or hammer your brother or your sister at any time whatsoever no matter who started what or who looked at whom in a manner that clearly and inarguably was a proposal to pummel. Do answer me in a clear and reasonable tone when I ask such forthright questions as: Did you pick up the wet towel from the floor or Have you studied for your history and science tests or Did you or did you not commit an egregious foul upon the corporal person of your brother? Do not leap upon, roll upon, do somersaults upon, do jumping-jacks upon, conduct wrestling matches upon, eat, or use any type of writing or coloring implement upon any bed, chair, couch, table, or counter in the house. Do learn to dribble and shoot the basketball with your left hand because being able to dribble and shoot with both hands is a rare and precious skill and may lead to a professional career that will keep us from the aforementioned peeling of mice in the poorhouse. Do not cut a guy at the knees while playing football because in my experience that leads to bruises in colors even your mother the painter has not imagined in the most feverish of her brilliant dreams. Do get a haircut once a decade on general principle because I say so and I am the dad. Do not think that I have any serious and final answers to any of the serious and pressing questions of life but do know that I love you with a love ferocious and inarticulate and thorough and mysterious and tidal and always will love you even when you have not as yet picked up the wet towel on the floor which if you do not pick that up soon I am going to roar in such a manner that birds in faraway countries will startle and wonder what has shivered the air beneath their holy and extraordinary wings.

Any questions?

# JOURNAL: ASH STREET

On my street the chestnut trees by the creek all let go at once and there is a steady rain of hard fruit the size of tennis balls. People move their cars. On windy days my children and I amble down the street and watch from a safe distance as the nuts leap from the trees. We take home handfuls and rot off the fruit and burnish the lovely brown seeds and my young sons throw them at each other and at their sister until I insist they desist and put the boys to bed but not the sister who is a teenager and so never sleeps. I work the nuts through my fingers like fat oily coins and consider the parallels between chestnuts and children. Both are wrapped in soft pebbly skins. Both have stubborn centers. Both gleam when polished. Both get crushed by cars. Both are subject to rot. Crows are fascinated by both.

———

Ash Street no longer has ash trees, although it does have alder, cedar, cherry, chestnut, fir, hazelnut, holly, locust, maple, oak, pine, redwood, spruce, walnut, and willow, and what dollops of sunlight and rain are not gobbled by the trees are sucked hungrily by blackberry and laurel thickets, some of the legs of the laurels as thick as my thigh.

———

Ash Street bisects a hill named for a man who was born in County Clare in Ireland. He took ship to America and landed in New York and walked to Nebraska (walked to Nebraska, the miles reeling by under his feet through JerseyPennsylvaniaOhioIndianaIllinoisIowa, resting here and there in some dusty summer village, Bee or Boone or Burr or Beaver, or in some cool river, the Platte or the Turkey or the Frenchman) where he joined that state's Second Cavalry Regiment and fought in the Civil War and then walked to Oregon, where he lived on our hill until the day he died. He was a stonemason. He died about noon, with a chisel in his hand.

———

Holy place in my old house on Ash Street: the infinitesimal indent made by fifteen years of left hands as woman and man and children leaned against the wall while adjusting the thermostat with their right hands.

———

Down the street lives the crazy lady, who occasionally walks through our back door and into our kitchen and stays for a long time, talking loudly. She tells everyone that her husband is traveling on business when actually he left permanently ten years ago. A while ago she leased her house to a young couple, telling them that she was moving to Egypt, but she has yet to leave and is still living in their basement.

———

A young couple appears at our back door to ask us to sign a petition to allow them to build a shed on what was an old right-of-way, as their yard was once a trail that led to the village smelter. The smelter and foundry and blast furnace where the first steel west of the Rockies was made are gone, but the legal means of approaching them with horse teams remains. I say to the young woman don't you like the fact that the ghosts of horses walk through your yard? and she says, uh, no.

———

At the west end of Ash Street is a poker and drinking cabin for a group of men and their dogs. It's surrounded now, very nearly grown over, by vast blackberry and laurel thickets; the men park their pickup trucks in a dell carved out of the thickets for their trucks and haul their beer and whiskey up the muddy steps into the cabin. At night you can hear music and laughter. Once a gunshot.

---

Animals seen on Ash Street: coyotes, deer, raccoons, hawks, herons, swifts, swallows, jays, flickers, once a policeman's horse, complete with leathery policeman.

---

Down the street there is a creek that had no official name until 1972, when the then-mayor named it Lost Dog Creek because when his two wolfhounds ran away he could always find them there. His wife says he should rename the creek Found Dog Creek but he only smiles.

---

One time I went to get the paper early in the morning on Ash Street and found a small boy smiling and silent, his diaper sagging. I recognized him; he was the toddler son of a young couple down the street. We stared at each other. The sun struggled over the rim of the world. I asked him what he was doing there shirtless and shoeless at dawn and he smiled. I walked him home and presented him to his mother. She made high shrill noises in her throat; I remember that.

---

Another time I went to get the mail when it was November in my soul and after reaching into the dark maw of the mailbox and finding nothing whatsoever I walked down Ash Street and into the dense laurel thicket by the poker cabin and sat there in the patient dark for a long time, listening to the thrum and rustle.

———

Other times: I saw a teenager sleeping in his army jacket in a blackberry thicket. I saw a woman praying by the creek. I saw a father slap his son's face. I saw a man throw a coffee cup at a dog. I found a baby picture in the mud. An old lady died across the street and when a neighbor told me of her death I realized I didn't even know her first name and we had been neighbors for more than a year.

———

Before Ash Street was a street it was a path with no name, running cheerfully above a creek with a name. Before it was a path it was probably a trail for the people who lived here, the people who called the lake below Waluga, the Place of Swans, and before it was a trail maybe it was a tunnel forced by burly deer through fern and fir, and before it was a tunnel maybe it was a tiny path for tiny animals, and before that, before there were any animals, before there were plants, before there was any green vibrant eager pulse and throb at all in the world, maybe it was a strip and stripe of stone; just like it is now.

# THE SENATOR

Went for a walk in the woods the other day with my mama, holding hands and moving slow through the dappled riot, stopping every few moments to rest. The woods were moist and dense and thrilled with butterflies. Tiny lizards skittered among palmetto fronds and we saw a toad the size of a dime. My children galloped away on the wooden walkway through the mud but I walked with my mama holding her hand because her hand is all papery now and something about her amused voice in my ear made me so unaccountably happy that I could hardly speak.

We were going to visit the Senator. The Senator is a cypress tree more than three thousand years old. He might be the biggest cypress tree in the world. He has a trunk as big around as a cottage. He is more than a hundred feet tall. He used to be almost two hundred feet tall but a lightning bolt knocked off his head which is why he wears a lightning rod now. You can see the copper wire along his trunk like a glinting vein if you squint a little.

We sat together at the foot of the Senator, my mama and me, squinting a little, and she told me stories, and butterflies lurched by, and quicksilver lizards posed and sprinted, and my children rumbled and burbled, and we contemplated the Senator, who set his roots as the first pyramids rose, and was king of the woods when Shakyamuni attained understanding and Yesuah was born and Muhammed rode to heaven on the great horse Buraq, whose name means lightning.

Lightning had hit the Senator pretty hard, we could see, because his trunk, which is a truly stunning amount of wood, just stopped abruptly, waaay up there, and now the Senator is topped with a scraggly raft of eager branches like green dreadlocks. Yet despite the ravages of time the Senator has the sort of dignity taught only by endurance, and we sat quietly, my mama and me, and contemplated his story.

Storks and egrets and herons have slept in him, and owls and warblers and thrushes, and vast troops of exuberant insects, and around his knobby knees have been otters and minks and bears, and frogs and turtles and salamanders, and in the old days there were jaguars and sloths and armadillos as big as cars, but these days mostly there are children, some dismissive but some agape, and lizards. There were a lot of lizards on the Senator, we noticed, some brown and some green and one with a blue tail and really cool yellow racing stripes.

My mama is not as tall as she used to be, either, and a lot of wild children have lived in and around her over the years, and she has seen many wars and weathers, but she has never been hit by lightning yet, although she has had epiphanies and seen miracles, pretty much every minute if you are paying attention, she says, which is what she has taught me to do, among other lessons, so after we finished our audience with the Senator we attended to the children, and herded them up and sent them thundering back up the wooden walkway, and then we followed them slowly, hand in hand, my mama telling stories and me so happy that for once I could not speak at all, which made my mama laugh, which is one of the loveliest sounds there ever was or will be.

# [SILENCE]

My sister stayed silent for several days when we were young. She was perhaps twenty years old, a student of spirituality. I was thirteen, a student of surliness. She announced that she would be silent for a while and then commenced to be so.

My parents were pretty graceful about it.

Seems like there's a lot more room in the house now, said my dad.

We should applaud and celebrate this form of prayer, said my mom.

Cooool, said my brothers. Is this permanent?

———

Eventually my sister spoke again — to yell at me, as I recall — but I never forgot those days. I was reminded of it recently when she emerged from a very long silence at the monastery where she now lives, and I asked her what her first words were when she emerged from her silent retreat, and she grinned and said pass the butter, which I did, which made her laugh, because those actually *were* her first words after retreat.

I *really* wanted that butter, she says.

Is it hard to be silent? I ask.

In the beginning it is, she says. Then it becomes a prayer.

———

I contemplate snippets of silence in mine existence and find them few; but I find that this delights rather than dismays me, for the chaos and hubbub in my life, most of my sea of sound, are my children, who are small quicksilver russet testy touchy tempestuous mammals always underfoot in the understory, yowling and howling and weeping and chirping and teasing and shouting and moaning and laughing and singing and screaming and sneering and sassing and humming and snoring and wheezing and growling and muttering and mumbling and musing and so making magic music all the livelong day. Which is pretty cool; though it will not be permanent.

―――

But sometimes they are silent and I am a student of their silence: my teenage daughter absorbed in book or homework, curled in her chair like a cat in the thicket of her room; my sons asleep, their limbs flung to the four holy directions, their faces beatific, their bedclothes rippled hills and dells, their beds aswarm with socks and shirts and books and balls; or all three children dozing in the back seat of the car as we slide through the velvet night, their faces flashing cinematically in my mirror as streetlights snick by metronomically; or the way they sat together silently before the silent television one crystal morning, four years ago, and watched two flaming towers crumble down down down unto unthinkable unimaginable ash and dust. Silently the towers fell, on our television screen, and silently my children watched, the twin scars burning into their brains.

―――

I ask my sister questions.
    What did you do when you were silent?
    I *listened*, she says. I listened really hard.
    Did you make any noise at all?
    Sometimes I found myself humming, she says, but it wasn't any music I'd known before. Which is pretty interesting. Where does music come from that you never heard before?
    Good question, I say.

And I found, she says, that it was relatively easy to not talk to other people, but much harder not to talk to animals. Isn't that odd? Why would that be?

Another good question, I say.

We had peacocks and guinea fowl at the monastery then, she says, and I was sort of in charge of the birds, which we had for two reasons. The peacocks someone gave us, which we thought was a generous if unusual gift until we had them for a while, and we realized what loud vain foul mean evil creatures they are, at which point we all realized what sort of *sick* human being would deliberately *give* a peacock to another human being, it's a form of *punishment* to have peacocks around, they peck at you and screech and find ways to make your life miserable, but the guinea fowl, now, they're not mean, no, *that's* not their problem, *their* problem is that they are without doubt or debate the most unbe*liev*ably stupid creatures to ever walk the earth, so in*cred*ibly stupid that you wonder how in heaven's name they ever managed to survive as a species, and the times I really *really* wanted to talk had to do with those guinea fowl, who were just so mind*bogg*lingly stupid I wanted to shriek. I mean, if they were three feet away from the hen house, and somehow got turned around so they were facing away from the hen house, well, rather than have the slightest inclination or imagination to try turning a*round*, they would stand there sobbing and wailing because they were utterly lost in the wilderness. Ye gods. You'd have to physically pick them up and turn them around to face the hen house. You could almost see the delight on their faces as the hen house reappeared. There it is again! It's a miracle! Ye gods.

------

Let us consider silence as destination, ambition, maturity of mind, focusing device, filter, prism, compass point, necessary refuge, spiritual refreshment, touchstone, lodestar, home, natural and normal state in which let's face it we began our existence in the warm seas of our mothers, all those months when we did not speak, and swam in salt, and dreamed oceanic dreams, and heard the throb and hum of mother, and the murmur and mutter of father, and the distant thrum of a million musics waiting patiently for you to be born.

———

I rise early and apply myself to my daily reading. Herman Melville: *All profound things and emotions of things are preceded and attended by Silence, and Silence is the general consecration of the universe.* Thomas Merton: *A man who loves God necessarily loves silence.* Jorge Luis Borges: *Absolute silence is the creative energy and intelligence of eternal being.* Job: *I put my finger to my lips and I will not answer again.* Melville again, poetically pithy in the midst of the vast sea of his sentences: *Silence is the only Voice of our God.*

To which I can only say (silently) *amen.*

———

It's harder to be silent in summer than in winter, says my sister. It's harder to be silent in the afternoon than in the morning. It's hardest to be silent when eating with others. It's easy to be silent in the bath. It's easy to be silent in the bed. It's easiest to be silent near water, and easiest of all to be silent by the lips of rivers and seas.

———

The silence of chapels and churches and confessionals and glades and gorges, places that wait for words to be spoken in the caves of their ribs. The split second of silence before two people simultaneously burst into laughter. The pregnant pause. The hot silence of lovemaking. The stifling stifled brooding silence just before a thunderstorm unleashes itself wild on the world. The silence of space, the vast of vista. The crucial silences between notes, without which there could be no music; no yes without no.

———

I study the silence of my wife. Her silence when she upset; a silence I can hear all too well after twenty years of listening for it. Her riveted silence in chapel. Her silence rocking children all those thousands of hours in the dark, the curved maple chair murmuring, the hum of the heater, the rustle of fevered boy resting against the skin of the sea from which he came.

———

My sister was loud as a teenager, cigarettes and music and shrieking at her brothers, but she gentled as the years went by, and much of my memory of her has to do with her sitting at the table with my mother, the two women talking quietly, the swirl of cigarette smoke circling, their voices quick and amused and circling, the mind of the mother circling the mind of the daughter and vice versa, a form of play, a form of love, a form of literature.

———

I rise earlier and earlier in these years. I don't know why. Age, sadness, a willingness to epiphany. Something is opening in me, some new eye. I talk less and listen more. Stories wash over me all day like tides. I walk through the bright wet streets and every moment a story comes to me, people hold them out to me like sweet children, and I hold them squirming and holy in my arms, and they enter my heart for a while, and season and salt and sweeten that old halting engine, and teach me humility and mercy, the only lessons that matter, the lessons of the language I most wish to learn; a tongue best spoken without a word, without a sound, with your hands clasped in prayer and your heart as naked as a baby.

# THEIR THIN BONY SHOULDERS

Some time ago I gave a characteristically rambling talk to a group of Benedictine nuns at their monastery in Oregon, beautifully and aptly named Mount Angel. As usual I set out to tell stories and sing prayers and tell jokes and draw tears and foment cheerful chaos and try to connect at some deep inexplicable level that I don't understand and can't explain that has everything to do with laughing and weeping which are of course extraordinary forms of prayer, and as usual I was granted more epiphany and delight than I could have ever delivered, which happens to me all the time, which is one of the reasons I feel like the richest man on earth, even though my back is sore all the time and my wife is a confusing country and my children *never* make their beds and it rains so much here that everyone gets a little mossy come winter.

Anyway, I'd arrived early at the monastery and wandered around the grounds for a couple of hours, out of respect for my hosts, trying to see and sense something of their lives and loves, their salty days, the way the wind slid through their fir trees, the geometry of the gravestones in their tiny cemetery, the way the hop fields and vineyards stretch away in corduroy rows beneath their little hill, the keening of hawks overhead, the secret words that dragonflies and damselflies spell in the air among the old stone buildings. I wandered and wondered. I walked the simple Stations of the Cross someone had carved in trees along a path. I examined the old wash house, where millions of prayers had been murmured over socks and frocks during the last century. I sat in the tall grass and prayed quietly for all sorts of things, even for the one-eyed cat glaring at me balefully from the brambles, and then I went to give my talk.

But first there was a meal, of course, and before the meal there were prayers, and the three nuns offering prayers were a microcosm of the monastery. One was very old and bent and grinning and calm. The second, the prioress, was tall and strong and commanding and gentle. The third was tiny and lithe and exuberant and looked to be about twenty years old. Each was terse and eloquent, and all three were funny, joking about making and selling thousands of jars of their legendary mustard, joking about the monastery's legendary basketball team in the old days, joking about their legendary battles against blackberry brambles which they fought valiantly even while thanking the merciful Lord for the berries, the black honey of summer as the great poet Mary Oliver says.

During dinner I talked to all sorts of nuns — postulants and novices, sisters who had taken first vows, sisters who had taken perpetual vows. I talked for a long while with a cheerful woman who when young had been a sister at the monastery but finally stepped away to spend her life as a teacher but never stopped visiting or supporting the monastery and in fact had been crucial in raising a million dollars for the new chapel. I talked to one young woman who was, as she said, an inquirer, a formal designation given to a woman who wished to acquaint herself with the Benedictine monastic community on the off chance that she might join up. Each of these women was quick-witted and humorous, but there was a calm about them, a direct ease, a warm dignity, that seemed to me, thinking about it later, best captured by the word grace.

Finally I gave my talk, singing and roaring, spinning stories, making jokes. I told them about barking point it down! at my toddler twin sons when I was teaching them The Guy Rules years ago, and about how the puppy knew a hundred words but just could not seem to get her head around the word no!, and about my friend Tommy who was roasted to white ash on forever-haunted September 11, and my theory that every story I tell about Tommy is a prayer for his brilliant soul and a dart to the heart of the coward who cowered in a cave, and I told stories of priests and firemen and dads and other brave men, and osprey and daughters and rivers and other miracles, and I tried to make those nuns and their friends laugh and cry, because laughter and tears are prayers too, and finally I concluded my burble and rant by telling them about my mama, the salt sea from whom I came.

---

She never turned aside a poor or hungry soul, did my mama, and she patiently taught children at home and in school for years and years, and she has the sharpest and quickest of wits and tongues, does my mama the deft storyteller, my mother with her fingers in the deep holy loam and skin of the earth, my mother who loves the smoky magical theater and miracle of the Mass, my mother with the memory of twenty elephants and a mind far quicker and more capacious than all of her children put together, my mother with a ferocious commitment to peace and justice and honest talk especially in the political and religious arenas where lies kill people and bleed souls, my mother who has not a jot nor an iota of pious nonsense in her, my mother who thinks that the divisions among Christian faiths are silly and stupid, my mother who knows more about the New Testament than I ever will and is fond of quoting the line wherein children are told to care for their fathers even when their minds go, which used to make my dad laugh in the other room, my mother stubborn as ten mules, my mother who took all her stunning talents and bent them toward love, and celebrating and living the wildly improbable message of the Christ, a message she thought could and should change the world, my mother who devoted her whole life to the possibility of that mad idea, my mother now near the end of her time on this God's earth, my mother soon to sift to dust, my mother more bent and fragile by the minute, my mother whose warm salty voice was the first thing I ever heard, and I cannot imagine a world without that grinning voice, a world without my mama in it.

———

And I stood there at the lectern, in that cavernous room in that lovely old monastery, with its cedared air like music in the nose, the extraordinary faces of the nuns held up to me in the twilight, and I tried to imagine or articulate or conceive a world without my mother in it, and I started to cry, and I could not stop.

Forty-nine years old, and still sobbing in front of nuns.

No one spoke.

After a couple of minutes I got a grip and looked out at those women and in the sweet silence, the brilliant shine of tears flashing here and there, I saw them for who they really are. I swear I did. I was granted and vouchsafed a vision: These sisters, and all sisters, are the sinews who hold the church together. Their prayers hold us like hands. The church has for centuries rested on their thin bony shoulders. They are brave beyond words and we take them for granted and we should get down on our creaky knees and clasp our hands in prayer and speak to the dust and say Lord we thank you for these women, for their grace we thank you, for their sacrifices and sweat we thank you, for their hearts in which we swim we thank you.

———

Look, I am not an idiot all the time, and I know full well, all too well, that the story of the world is struggle and sadness, loneliness and loss; but to my mind there just is no way to stay sad as long as there are thin bony brave women like these nuns, like my mom, like your mom, in the world. It just cannot be done. We cannot let ourselves despair at the greed and cruelty of the world, and sometimes of our church, because these sisters do not despair, they fight the brambles all day and night for us, and they are lodestars and compasses and prisms and leaders of the world that will come, the world of joy and light, where no child weeps from fear, where no one huddles hopeless.

If we are to properly honor and celebrate the legacy of such graceful and strong people as the sisters at Mount Angel, who have bent their whole lives to the promise that love would defeat darkness, then we must march into our days with rage and song, with hammers in our hands and prayers in our mouths, and build us a new church and a new world and a new roaring poem, with all the grace and strength and sweet wild magic we can muster. *It can be done.* It's being done as I write these words and as you read them. These brave women bet their lives on that premise. My mama bet her life on that premise. Are we to tell them they were wrong and the task is too big? I don't have the courage to tell my mother such a thing, for she is a tart tough tiny Irish Catholic woman from New York City, and even my brothers, strapping men far taller and broader than me, quail at the thought of telling our mum what cannot be done, and it would take a far braver man than me to stand up to tiny Sister Alicia and tell her the work she has chosen to do is a bust. She would laugh in my face, and she would be right.

So let us go then, you and I, and forge a new thing. We do not know its shape; but we know the astounding idea at its heart, the idea that has driven the Catholic clan through two thousand years, the idea that remains, I believe, the key to the moral evolution of the human race, the idea that fell again and again from the lips of the gaunt dusty man with starlight in his veins: love love love love love.

# THE NEXT ELEVEN MINUTES

I am not so stupid as to make any public comment whatsoever about the character and nature and music of my marriage, which I understand less about by the year anyway because my marriage, like every marriage that is or was or will be, is different from every other marriage, and my marriage changes shape every eleven minutes or so, and my marriage, like every marriage, is ultimately an utterly ephemeral thing, a shared idea, a mental and emotional construct which both parties believe in to varying degrees at the same time or else there you are at the bus stop muttering about how you used to be married. And also the person to whom I am married, or to whom I was married eleven minutes ago, is a mysterious changeable country whom I try to simply savor and appreciate rather than attempt to understand, or God help us all predict in any way shape or form whatsoever, such predilection to prediction being the surest road to muttering at the bus stop about the marriage you used to have.

Yet there have been many riveting moments in my marriage, and I recount them here cheerfully so that you can tell me what they mean, for I have no idea. Like when our three children were hauled wet and startled from the salt sea of her womb and I saw my wife's spleen and thin layer of subcutaneous fat, which I thought was pretty cool but she didn't. Or the time we lost a baby in utero. Or all the times she has fallen asleep on my shoulder watching movies and the way she wakes with a start and asks anxiously did she drool or snore? Or the way she becomes so absorbed in the paintings she paints that she loses track of the time and hoots with surprise when she realizes how late it is. Or she way she reads by the fire wrapped in a shawl. Or the way she forgets that the milk for her coffee is boiling and yelps with surprise every single morning when it boils over. Or the way she loves to work in the yard rain or sleet or shine. Or the way she laughs from the very fiber of her being sometimes with a dear friend on the phone.

Or the way she loses her temper sometimes suddenly and slashes and slices with a stunning tongue. Or the way she retires upstairs sometimes in tears overcome by exhaustion and rude children and unsubtle husband. Or the way our love affair has waxed and waned and ebbed and flowed and worn so many different coats of motley that sometimes I conclude it has died and sometimes I am agog that it has been born once again miraculously from ash.

Many times I have concluded that all marriages are nuts and my marriage is nuts but I find myself delighted by her company which is endlessly stimulating sometimes in ways beyond hilarity or sensuality and sometimes in ways so frustrating and heartrending that I go pray and walk and hum and fold laundry and recall that I am no gleaming glittering prize either, I am just a guy, muddled and humming.

I remember everything, I am memorious, that's my gift and my curse, and I remember the way her voice once came shivering out of the dusk, telling me about her dad who had just died whom she loved madly, she was his last child, his late-surprise baby daughter, and I remember the quiver of joy in her high-beam eyes as we danced on our wedding day, swinging each other so fast and wild that if either let go we'd still be orbiting Neptune, and I remember the million hours she has rocked and consoled and bandaged and fed and cleaned and snarled at and sang for our children, and the million hours we have wrassled ideas and locked limbs, and I know the sound of her sob and the lilt of her laugh, the lurch of her logic and the flare of her fury, yet after twenty years I know her hardly at all; which maybe is crucial for marriage as a verb, and why I am married, and why the most momentous moments of my marriage seem to me to be incontrovertibly and inarguably the next eleven, if they come, which I hope they will, I pray they will, though no one, including most of all me and my wife, knows if they will come, or what they will bring, which seems to me somehow the secret of the whole thing.

But what do I know?

# REC LEAGUE

Three years ago I volunteered to coach the grade school boys' basketball team in the local rec league here in Oregon. I did so for the usual reason men coach, because none of the other fathers would do it, even though I begged and sniveled and pleaded, but they all backed away slowly, their mouths filled with creative excuses, and as one guy said to me it was my moral responsibility to coach the boys because not one but two of the boys were my sons, so there.

So I coached, so to speak, that first year, and then again last year because none of the other fathers would do it and I had a year's experience anyway, and again this year because, heck, I have always been the coach for as long as anyone can remember, and partly as a way to try to stay sane I have kept notes about certain adventures and misadventures, like the time I started practice by making them run laps and then got into an interesting discussion with a dad about grilling fish and forgot about the boys until one of them threw up after running thirty laps, or the many times my players have been so excited they shot at the wrong basket, or the time my point guard used such foul and reprehensible language to the referee that we had to call two time-outs in a row we were laughing so hard, or the time we won ten games in a row and then lost a squeaker and I found out that the other coach had secretly scouted our team for the previous two weeks, or the time our center told me he couldn't play because a girl he had a crush on was in the gym and she was making him all nervous and everything, could I maybe ask her to leave? Or the time a crow hopped into the gym and everybody freaked out, or the time a player on another team got hit in the nose and burst into tears and walked out of the gym and walked home, or the time we only had four players but won the game anyway although I thought I was going to have to carry all four guys home after that, or the time a ref really and truly did swallow his whistle and the other ref had to take him to the hospital, or the time a player on another team put his cell phone in his jock and when a pass hit him amidships his phone rang, or how the first year I coached my guys were such rotten free-throw shooters that when one of the guys finally hit one halfway during the season we called time and everyone shook his hand, or the kid we had one year who could just *not* get the idea of dribbling the ball down pat and ran with it everywhere with his arm out like a running back fending off defenders, or the game we played one time that was as close to perfect as I think I will ever see on this wild sweet holy earth, my boys sprinting and cutting and whipping passes and driving to the hole and not taking wild shots and actually playing defense and hitting the boards in such vivacious creative energetic exuberant fashion that sometime during the second half I leaned back in my rickety folding chair in the echoing elementary-school gym and wanted to cry for reasons that remain murky to me.

There were other reasons to cry. One time I asked a boy if he had a basket at his house on which to practice his vague grasp of the idea of a layup and he said quietly there was a basket near all *three* of his houses, his mom's and his dad's and his grandma's. And there was a boy who had a black eye and bruises on his shoulders and he told me he fell down the stairs but when I asked him if his dad was coming to the game he winced. There was a boy whose mom and her new husband sat on one side of the gym and his dad and his new wife sat on the other and the son, a terrific ballplayer, never looked at either his mom or his dad but stared at me with fearsome eyes during timeouts. I could never bear to take him out of the game because it seemed to me that the game was the one place he was happy.

But mostly it's been hilarious and poignant. I have seen some of these boys grow more than a foot taller. I have spent hundreds of hours with them in all the elementary school gyms there are in our town. I have given speeches at the end of the season about their diligence and grace as I handed out tinny trophies that they love and will probably have all their lives. I have made them run and laugh, which are good things to do. They have made me listen to their horrendous thumping music which isn't as bad as I thought it would be. We have talked about politics and books and girls and burgers. They have brought me back into the bright redolent funk of gymnasiums and the cheerful tedium of practice and the quivering tension of games. They have brought me back to the sinuous quicksilver geometry of basketball, the most American of games, with its energy and violence and grace and joy and competitive drive, its swing and rhythm and music. They have trusted me and confided in me and wept as I knelt down and looked into their faces and did my best to calm them.

For a while they gave me the extraordinary gift of their company as they went from being goofy boys to lanky young men, and here at the end of the last season I'll ever coach I find myself savoring every shred and shard of the thing I didn't want to do three years ago. I sit back on my rickety chair and watch them, and the curious thing is that while occasionally now there is a flash of real creativity and grace, the very thing that you watch games for, those moments when brains and bodies flow, it's the egregious mistakes that I will miss the most — the ludicrous shot, the hopeless pass, the hilariously bad defense, the brain-lock moments. There was one last Saturday, when a kid got the ball, a new kid, a gentle sweet soul who never played the game before in his life, and he was so excited to actually have the ball and a clear lane to the basket that he ran delightedly to the wrong basket and scored. Everyone cheered and laughed and shook his hand and he blushed and the game flew on ancient and relentless but I sat there shivering with joy.

# A CHILD IS NOT A FURNITURE

One time when I lived in Chicago I spent an hour talking to a woman who was wearing a dress of the brightest red I have ever seen in all my born days and I have lived fifty years. This was on the Cicero Avenue bus at three in the morning. She said she was returning to the apartment where she lived with her husband. I inquired after children and she said,

My husband and I trying to welcome children but as yet we have not been blessed. I would like to have five children. I am myself one of five. My husband however an only child of complex circumstances. He have misgivings and forebodings. There are also financial considerations. But there are lots of kinds of considerations. I feel there is also spiritual consideration. My husband does not find a way to agree with this. He is a practical pragmatic man. This may be because of his circumstances. For example he say where the baby sleep? I say the baby will sleep with us. He have misgiving and foreboding. He says what if it twins? I say well then we blessed by twins. He cannot arrive at agreement. Now, people say to me I should just *have* the baby and then my husband will adjust to the baby. But this is dishonest. You cannot be dishonest with your husband. Otherwise why have a husband? What would be the point of a husband if you dodging the man? He is a good man despite his circumstances. He has risen mostly above his circumstances. Yet sometimes they drag him down. He measure and calculate. He arrange things just so. But you cannot arrange a child just so. A child is not a furniture. He says who discipline the child? I say we will do so together with the gentlest hand. He has misgiving. He worry things ahead of time. I admire that man fierce but you cannot worry all the time. You must ford the river with your head held high. He says where the boy go to school? I say the *girl* will go to the best school available to us at that time. He says money money. But money money is not the be all. If it was the be all then what is the point? The point is what you do *without* the money. The point is what you do with dash and brass. This is who you are. You are not what you can buy. That is silly talk. He says the reason we are with each other is because I fire and he ice. Some truth to that. I zest him up and he calm me down. We fit together very nice. But in the end two is just two. There is no place really to go after one plus one. At some point you have to be more than two. Now, there are many ways to be more than two. I know that and he know that. But he is careful and pragmatic. He take one step at a time and then look around weary for trouble. That is who he is. I cannot change him. I do wish a child is granted unto us. I would wish many a child. People say *pray* for the baby and the Lord will *provide* but that is not how things happen. You do not ask for things and you get the thing. The Lord is not a suggesting box. That is silly talk. The way it is is you dream a thing and work for a thing and make the way easy for it and then maybe that thing be born. *That* is how it happens. Some things I do know. Here is my stop and I will depart. Let us shake hands. Ford the river with your head held high.

# WHY DO WE SAY ONE THING
# ABOUT CHILDREN
# BUT DO ANOTHER?

Why is that? Because, as you know and I know, they are really and truly, no exaggeration and hyperbole whatsoever, The Future of the Planet. Because soon enough we will be in their grubby gentle hands and they will be making all the crucial decisions about clean water and wars and health care for decrepit ancient Us. Because we swore and vowed to every god we ever invented that we would care for them with every iota of our energy when they came to us miraculously from the sea of the stars. Because they are the very definition of innocent, and every single blow and shout and fear that rains down upon them is utterly undeserved and unfair and unwarranted. Because we used to *be* them, and we remember, dimly, what it was like to be small and frightened and confused.

We say one thing about children as a nation and a people and a species and we do another. We say they are the holy heart of our society and culture and we lie. We say the words *family values* like a cool slogan on a warm flag that wraps protectively around the smallest and newest of us but we let them starve and wither and be raped and live in the snarling streets. Because even the best of us, the mothers and fathers and teachers and nurses and doctors and counselors and nuns and coaches and other sweet patient souls who listen to children with their hearts, cannot hope to reach more than a few, and so many go unheard, unwitnessed, unmoored, unmourned. Because even the most cynical and weary of us in our iciest darkest moments has to laugh when we see a cheerful toddler trying to cram a peach up his nose, or an infant chatting amiably with a dog, or a tiny kid leaping over a tiny wave at the beach and being pretty proud that she showed *that* old ocean who was boss, yes she did!

Because if we are any shard or shred of the people we want to be as Americans and human beings we have *got* to take care of them before we do anything else at all, we have to coddle and teach them, and feed and clothe them, and nurse and doctor them, and house and hold them, and be patient as they thrash toward who they might be if they get enough light and water and song, even if, as they stumble through their teenage construction zones, they thrash mostly against those who love them most.

But you know and I know that for every two we raise decently, another is lost, that in Oregon alone there are thousands of them who did not eat today, who cannot go to the doctor, who have no bedroom, who hear no parent moaning about the dishes or growling about homework, who have no glimmering hopes, who have no gleaming dreams, and we sit in our offices and dens and legislative chambers and dicker and debate and issue proclamations and promises and meanwhile they starve and wither and are raped and live in the streets.

I know how incredibly hard most of us work on behalf of every kid we know. I know more brave and weary people breaking their backs for kids than I can count. But there are a lot of kids we don't help, lost kids, scared kids, kids who are headed to an ocean of blood and despair. How can we catch them on the beach? How can we bend the bruised and blessed world and save them? Because they're all our kids. And all they want, all they ever wanted, is us.

# ALL LEGS & CURIOSITY

In the back of the cavernous echoing convocation for shy freshmen at the college dipping their toes into the roaring river of campus life for the first time there were also of course a raft of outwardly calm but inwardly rattled parents of every gender, and I got to talking to a tiny mother, and as soon as she started talking about her daughter she burst into tears, right there by the women's bathroom, but she recovered fast, and started talking faster, and I think you should hear what she said: This is the greatest moment and the worst moment. I was just changing her diapers a moment ago. Now she's all legs and curiosity. I can't believe she's not coming home tonight. I'll get ready to send her a text message at midnight *where are you come on home* and she won't come home. She'll be here with you all. I love that. I can't bear that. Her father can't stop crying. He's out in the truck. Everyone thinks he's a tough businesslike guy and he's crying in the truck. These are our *babies*. All these tall babies. Will you take care of her? Will you know if she's sad and scared? She's scared more than she admits. She brought her baby blanket, you know. In the bottom of her luggage. She doesn't think I know but I know. I held it against my face and it smelled like her and I cried and cried. I hope you know how great she is. She's the greatest kid in the history of the world. She wanted to come here so badly. The day the letter came she danced right out the front door and across the grass and around the neighborhood waving the letter at the neighbors and everyone was laughing and pouring out of their houses to give her a hug because everybody loves her. You'll love her too; you'll see. You better take care of her. She didn't want to go anywhere else. We tried to be sensible but she wouldn't hear of it. She knew this was the place for her. She knew she would get in. She knew you would know. She never wears socks. She'll get sick twice this year, mark my words. October and February. Are you writing that down? Can you tell the nurses here?

She wants to be a nurse. Her grandmother was a nurse. My husband's mother. He's still out in the truck. He says he'll be fine by dinner. He won't be fine by dinner. He used to carry her on his back all the time when she was little. They would climb mountains that way. He makes fish just the way she likes it. He says he's going to go talk to your chefs here about how they cook fish. She'll be the best nurse there ever was. She has the biggest heart of anyone God ever made in a million years. I can't stand it that she's not coming home tonight. She's not coming home as a kid ever again, is she? Will you take the very best care of her you can? Do you swear? Because I spent every minute of every day since she was born thanking God for the gift of that kid, and even when she was bad she was the best kid there ever was. Promise me you'll take care of her. I can't bear this. You'll know her — she's tall with long hair and blue jeans and a smile like the sun. You can't miss her. When you meet her you'll know who she is. You'll *know*. Trust me. Once you meet her you'll never forget her for the rest of your life. Trust me when I say that. Trust me.

# II.

# COOL THINGS

As a fan's notes for grace, and quavery chant against the dark, and hoorah from the hustings, I sing a song of things that make us grin and bow, that just for an instant let us see sometimes the web and weave of merciful, the endless possible, the incomprehensible inexhaustible inexplicable *yes*.

Such as, for example, to name a few,

The way the sun crawls over the rim of the world every morning like a child's face rising beaming from a pool all fresh from the womb of the dark, and the way jays hop and damselflies do that geometric aeroamazing thing and bees inspect and birds probe and swifts chitter, and the way the young mother at the bus-stop has her infant swaddled and huddled against her chest like a blinking extra heart, and the way a very large woman wears the tiniest miniskirt with a careless airy pride that makes me so happy I can hardly squeak, and the way seals peer at me owlishly from the surf like rubbery grandfathers, and the way cormorants in the ocean never *ever* get caught by onrushing waves but disappear casually at the last possible second so you see their headlong black stories written on the wet walls of the sea like moist petroglyphs, and the way no pavement asphalt macadam concrete cement thing can ultimately defeat a tiny relentless green thing, and the way people sometimes lean eagerly facefirst into the future, and the way infants finally discover to their absolute agogishment that those fists swooping by like tiny fleshy comets are *theirs!*, and the way when my mom gets caught unawares by a joke she barks with laughter so infectious that people grin two towns over, and the way one of my sons sleeps every night with his right leg hanging over the side of his bed like an oar no matter how many times I fold him back into the boat of the bed, and the way our refrigerator hums to itself in two different keys, and the way the new puppy noses through hayfields like a headlong exuberant hairy tractor, and the way my daughter always makes one immense final cookie the size of a door when she makes cookies, and the way one son hasn't had a haircut since Napoleon was emperor, and the way crows arrange themselves sometimes on the fence like the notes of a song I don't know yet, and the way car engines sigh for a few minutes after you turn them off, and the way your arm goes all totally nonchalant when you are driving through summer with the window down, and the way people touch each other's forearms when they are scared, and the way every once in a while someone you hardly know says something so piercingly honest that you want to just kneel down right there in the grocery store near the pears, and the way little children fall asleep with their mouths open like fish, and the way sometimes just a sidelong glance from someone you love makes you all shaky for a second before you can get your mask back on, and the way some people when they laugh tilt their heads way back like they need more room for all the hilarity in their mouths, and the way hawks and eagles always look so *annoyed*, and the way people shuffle daintily on icy pavements, and the way churches smell dense with hope, and the way that men's pants bunch up at the knees when they stand after kneeling in church, and the way knees are gnarled, and the way faces curve around the mouth and eyes according to how many times you smiled over the years, and the way people fall asleep in chairs by the fire and snap awake startled and amazed, unsure, just for a second, what planet exactly they are on, which is a question we should probably all ask far more often than we do.

Look, I know very well that brooding misshapen evil is everywhere, in the brightest houses and the most cheerful denials, in what we do and what we have failed to do, and I know all too well that the story of the world is entropy, things fly apart, we sicken, we fail, we grow weary, we divorce, we are hammered and hounded by loss and accidents and tragedies. But I also know, with all my hoary muddled heart, that we are carved of immense confusing holiness; that the whole point for us is grace under duress; and that you either take a flying leap at nonsensical illogical unreasonable ideas like marriage and marathons and democracy and divinity, or you huddle behind the wall. I believe that the coolest things there are cannot be measured, calibrated, calculated, gauged, weighed, or understood except sometimes by having a child patiently explain it to you, which is another thing that should happen far more often to us all.

In short I believe in believing, which doesn't make sense, which gives me hope.

# MUTE, RIVEN, BLESSED

I see them all the time. Naked white crosses on the shoulder of the road, on the other side of the ditch, at that bad curve on the highway.

There's one on a high riverbank where a kid drove off into the river and the car sank bubbling and they found him blue a day later.

There's one near the beach where two lanes merge into one but if you are drunk and driving too fast through the utter darkness of the ancient forest you maybe miss the merge and you hit a fir tree bigger than a house and you turn into past tense, cold meat, a story people remember.

There's one on the most innocent farm road you ever saw where nobody should ever have an accident but a girl did one bright afternoon and no one knows why.

There are four of them all together like a silent tiny white forest: four kids roasted when their car flipped and rolled and burned. The grass was black there for the longest time.

And I live in Oregon, where a spontaneous shrine grew and grew and grew by the school fence at Thurston High School in the old timber town of Springfield in 1998 after a fifteen-year-old kid named Kip Kinkel shot his mother to death and his father to death and then walked into school with two guns in the morning and opened fire and murdered two kids, Mikael Nickolauson and Ben Walker, and wounded twenty-five other kids before a wrestler named Jake tackled him. In the days after blood trickled along the white polished hallways of Thurston High School thousands of people walked to the chain-link fence outside the school and tied things to the fence: photographs, flowers, balloons, quilts, a commencement gown and cap, notes, verses from the Bible, every conceivable form of prayer and mourning and memory. The shrine stayed there for weeks and weeks and weeks. No one had the heart to order it dismantled. People came all day and night to that hole in the world where prayers went up into the sky like a river of tears. The fence is still there, naked now, and a friend tells me people still stop at it day and night and pray. A chain-link chapel, open to the elements, soaked in rain and rue.

---

I do not ask why we do this, why we erect little white crosses and signs and mounds of flowers and cairns of stones where people died. We *know* why we do this. We cannot *not* do this. We mark the spot where the soul left the body and returned to Sender. These places are holy. They are holes wrenched open suddenly, often in flame, doors through which a soul has passed from this world. To me they are holier than any church, in the same way a mother's belly is holier than any church, because those sweet bellies and those roasted holes in the grass are where souls entered and left this intricate realm; they are places of mercy and mystery; they are the portals from which the created emerges and through which the created departs.

Hospital beds, ambulance gurneys, wet ditches in wars, seething smoking holes where gargantuan buildings were destroyed by murderers in airplanes, quiet bedrooms in quiet houses, icy mountain ledges, howling seas, serene back gardens while digging in the compost — we die everywhere and everywhere that spot is henceforth holier than before, to us anyway; we do not spend much time thinking about the deaths of the million infinitesimal creatures with which we share the land, but they die too, ebbing away in tiny tides, their unique and miraculous sparks drawn home into a coherent energy and love we only dimly sense, here and there; such sensual experiences being sacraments — the moments when you feel divine breath in your ear and fingers on your face.

---

We are alone, each and all of us, even as we swim in the ocean of love and grace that is our joyous work here; and we will die alone, each of us, leaving our bodies behind at some moment brooding in the future. And bed or beach, highway or hospice, those who love us will mark that spot, and then mark the spot where our bones are laid to rest or ashes swirled into the thirsty sea — as I mark the spots where girls and boys and infants and women and men have died along the roads here, the naked white crosses, the flowers and flags.

Once, there, in those spots, something left the earth. The words we have are so thin. Life, soul, the miraculous energy that drives bone and meat toward love and light, the electric prayer of her, the hymn of him: gone.

But not gone. Is there a wilder, crazier, truer belief than that?

And if life is a miraculous opening, why cannot death be a miraculous opening also?

So those thin naked white crosses in the rain, that dripping chain-link fence at Thurston High: maybe they are not exits, after all. Maybe they are the holiest doors. Maybe they are not holes where something emptied out. Maybe they are holes through which something pours in. A love so far beyond our ken that we can only stand there mute, riven, blessed.

# ON MIRACULOUSNESS

A while ago I was shuffling along the roaring shore of the misnamed Pacific Ocean, humming to myself, pondering this and that and the other, when I saw a crippled kid hopping toward me. She was maybe four years old and her feet were bent so sideways that her toes faced each other so she scuttled rather than walked. I never saw a kid crippled quite like that before. I thought for a minute she was alone but then I noticed the rest of her clan, a big guy and two other small girls, probably the dad and sisters, walking way ahead of the crippled kid.

The crippled kid was cheerful as a bird and she zoomed along awfully fast on those sideways feet. She was totally absorbed in the seawrack at the high tide line — shards of crab and acres of sand fleas and shreds of seaweed and ropes of bullwhip kelp and fractions of jellyfish and here and there a deceased perch or auklet or cormorant or gull, and once a serious-sized former fish that looked like it might have been a salmon. In the way of all people for a million years along all shores she stared and poked and prodded and bent and pocketed and discarded, pawing through the loot and litter of the merciless musing sea.

She was so into checking out tide-treasure that her dad and sisters got waaay out ahead of her and after a while the dad turned and whistled and the crippled kid looked up and laughed and took off hopping faster than you could ever imagine a kid that crippled could hop, and when she was a few feet away from the dad he crouched a little and extended his arm behind him with his hand out to receive her foot, and she shinnied up his arm as graceful and quick as anything you ever saw, and she slid into what must have been her usual seat on his neck and off they went, the sisters pissing and moaning about having to wait for the crippled kid and the dad tickling the bottoms of the kid's feet, so that I heard the kid laughing fainter and fainter as they receded, until finally I couldn't hear her laughing anymore, but right about then I was weeping like a child anyways, at the intricate astounding unimaginable inexplicable complex thicket of love and pain and suffering and joy, at the way that kid rocketed up her daddy's arm quick as a cat, at the way he crouched just so and opened his palm so his baby girl could come flying up the holy branch of his arm, at the way her hands knew where to wrap themselves around his grin, at the way the sisters were all snarling about the very same kid sister that if anyone else ever grumbled about her they would pound him silly, and this is all not even to mention the glory of the sunlight that day, and the basso moan of mother sea, and the deft-diving of the little black sea-ducks in the surf, and the seal popping up here and there looking eerily like my grandfather, and the eagle who flew over like a black tent heading north, and the extraordinary fact that the Coherent Mercy granted me my own kids, who were not crippled, and were at that exact moment arguing shrilly about baseball at the other end of the beach.

I finally got a grip and set to shuffling again, but that kid stays with me. Something about her, the way she was a verb, the way she was happy even with the dark cards she was dealt, the way she loved openly and artlessly, the way even her sisters couldn't stay mad but had to smile when she shinnied up their daddy's arm, seems utterly holy to me, a gift, a sign, a reminder, a letter from the Light.

*In my Father's house are many mansions,* said the thin confusing peripatetic rabbi long ago, a line I have always puzzled over, yet another of the man's many zen koans, but I think I finally have a handle on that one. What he meant, did Yesuah ben Joseph of the haunting life and message, is that we are given gifts beyond measure, beyond price, beyond understanding, and they mill and swirl by us all day and night, and we have but to see them clearly, for a second, to believe wholly in the bounty and generosity and mercy of *I Am Who Am.*

I am not stupid *all* the time, and I saw how crippled that kid was, and I can only imagine her life to date and to come, and the tensions and travails of her family, and the battles she will fight and the tears she will shed, and I see and hear the roar of pain and suffering in the world, the floods and rapes and starvings and bullets, and I am too old and too honest not to admit how murderous and greedy we can be. But I have also seen too many kids who are verbs to not believe we swim in an ocean of holy. I have seen too many men and women and children of such grace and humor and mercy that I know I have seen The Holy Thing ten times a day. I think maybe you know that too and we just don't talk about it much because we are tired and scared and the light flits in and around so much darkness. But there was a crippled kid on the beach and The Holy Thing in her came pouring out her eyes and I don't forget it.

*In my Father's house are many mansions,* said the skinny Jewish guy, confusingly, and then in his usual testy editorial way, *if it were not so, I would have told you,* and then, in a phrase I lean on when things go dark, *I go to prepare a place for you.*

But we are already in the doorway of that house, don't you think?

# PONG PING

I met a man recently who told me his name was Pong Ping, and yes, he said gently, I am aware that in this country there is a certain, what do you say, humorous resonance to my name, yet it is my actual real name, given to me by my mother, and I wear it with pride. My name was not a source of amusement generally until I came to this country, at age seventeen, to attend college.

I was born and raised in Hong Kong, the child of a devout Buddhist family, but for social reasons I was educated by the Sisters of Saint Paul of Chartres, and so arrived at a familiarity and growing interest in Christianity, which seems to me, even at my young age, to be the closest of cousins with Buddhism. I have read your Thomas Merton quite closely, and I believe that he too saw not mere similarity but, shall we say, a resonance between the two faith traditions.

Both are devoted to the holiness of what is, the divine genius of creation; both are absorbed in attentiveness as the beginning of all prayer, as your great poet Mary Oliver says; and both are committed to the belief that every moment is heavy with miracle, if only we had the eyes to see.

And both are founded on the conviction that there is an unquenchable spark of holy fire in the breast of every human being, that no human being is beyond redemption, that no matter what acts you have committed, no matter what your crime, there is forgiveness possible, there is a light shining out of the deepest darkness.

I believe that this is genius.

I have the most firmly held conviction that these things are true, and that thousands of years of belief in these things, by millions of people, are incontrovertible evidence of their veracity. I have the greatest respect for religious authority, for my elders in faith and tradition, but I am also very aware, as a man who has lived now some years in America, that no authority can tell me what to think and what to believe; this independence of mind and spirit seems like the admirable essence of the American character, although you yourselves note that it can be taken too far, and end in anarchy and selfishness; but for me an education in independence of mind has only made me more convinced of the truth of the Christian and Buddhist traditions, which, more than any other religions I have studied, are alert to the profligate generosity of creation.

Additionally both traditions seem to me to be the most honest and understanding of the nature of suffering, that suffering is the price we pay for existence in this realm, and that while suffering in and of itself has no redeeming value, the grace with which we bear our crosses, and the generosity with which we shoulder the burden of the crosses of others, is active prayer and active gratitude for the extraordinary gift of life in this realm.

It seems to me that people generally spend far too much time thinking and arguing about the things that are different between and among religious traditions, and far too little time in amazement at the things that are, shall we say, resonant between and among them. So, for example, to debate the doctrine of reincarnation, as against a belief in the possibility of being reunited with the Creator immediately after death, seems to me rather a waste of time and energy better spent in appreciation of the many paths to enlightenment shared by Buddhism and Christianity. I would suggest that energy used in this way is perhaps a better use of the time we have in this realm, time which ideally should be spent in celebration and working toward, shall we say, a higher plane of existence. Even at this young age I believe that working toward the next stage is the work that has clearly been assigned to us. In college and in graduate school I studied anthropology and paleontology, and my belief is that human beings are evolving toward some higher plane of existence. It seems to me that here too perhaps religions, in their visionary ways, have looked dimly into the future and seen what may come to pass, which is why in both Buddhist and Christian traditions there are firm beliefs in transitory beings between human beings and the One — various orders of angels, in Christianity, and various stages of enlightenment, in Buddhism.

I have very much enjoyed this conversation, said Pong Ping finally, but it is now eight o'clock, and I am due at work in thirty minutes, and it takes twenty-two minutes to walk from here to the school where I work. I pray for your joy and the peace of the One.

# THE YOU OF YOU

A guy who works in a hospital is a nurse. A lot of babies are born who don't live a day, he says, but of course their parents name them, and I keep a list. There was a woman who named her son Once. He lived an hour. There was a boy named Chance and a boy named Jesus and a girl named Wonderful. We had a stillborn baby the parents named Almost. One man named his daughter Lost. Some people name their children after trees and birds and such: Ash and Pine and Hawk and Wren. We have had several Rivers and one Ocean. A lot of names have something to do with music, like Harmony and Melody, and a lot of them have to do with light and color and natural phenomena like Rainbows and Sunshine and Summer. A lot of the babies don't get any names at all because they die so fast and the mother is exhausted and despairing and we don't press the matter. Those are the babies who are named A and B and such in the records. Baby Boy A, Baby Girl B. We name them quietly ourselves, though. If you look at their faces long enough their names arrive. Maybe those are the names the babies are really supposed to have. You never know. I think every child born has a name just as every child born has a character and a personality that was never in the world before and never will be again. Me personally I think that when you are formed in your mother's womb you have a name that is part of every cell in your body. You *are* your name. Your name isn't a word or even a sound. It's the you of you. I am not being articulate but you know what I mean. You stare at a baby, you know, a child who has been dead for half an hour, a child who was alive when she came out of her mother, and who she was, maybe who she *is*, and her name appears in your mind. A friend of mine says you hear the name in your heart like the ringing of a bell but that seems too poetic and fanciful to me for what really happens, which is that somehow after a while you just somehow know her name. I go write it down so it doesn't get lost. We keep the list private, just something among us working here, something important in ways that are hard to explain. Hey, you're a writer, *you* write it down and try to explain it. I can't. I just know it really matters somehow to listen for what her name is and then write it down. Somehow that's what I am supposed to do. There are a lot of things we are supposed to do that are really important in ways we will never understand but we do them anyway, right?

# THE WORD

In the beginning was the word, no? Not corralled electricity, not digital display, not ephemeral flicker on a stupendous screen. In the beginning was the word, and *kai theos en ho logos,* the word was God, the Coherent Mercy speaking everything into being, forming from that unimaginable imagination an endless story, giving birth to it from the holy cave of that unthinkable mouth, so that even now, billions of years later, the words we use, the tools of our tongues, are shards of holiness, glittering and loaded with that original light; as we remember sometimes when a string of them fits together and opens a heart.

The first words my daughter ever read were words printed on the spine of a book. I was there. It was evening. She was four years old. She ran her fingers along the spine of the book and sounded out the syllables and suddenly put them together into words and her mother and I sat there agape and my heart shivered and our daughter turned and grinned and nothing was ever quite the same.

We used to carve words into stones and tablets. We still do. We wrote them on the skins of calves and sheep and antelope and bison. We still do. Now we also write them on paper made of oak and maple and pine and spruce. We write them on cotton and linen and silk. We write them in sand. We write them in the air. We use our fingers and toes and sticks and pens and pencils and quills and markers and crayons and brushes and styluses and any and every tool that comes to hand to make letters, the loops and swirls and darts and corners of the word. Such a sensual act. Such a sacrament.

For all that we spend our days snuffling and rooting for information, trafficking and trading in it, milling and shilling, wired for hire, what we crave most is touch, warmth, skin, joy, hope. So we tell each other stories as a way to extend the hands of our hearts. We use our words and hands and mouths to tell stories. Mark these words: as the century gets ever more electronic and virtual and remote, we will ever more turn to the tactile, the actual, to wood and wool, stone and bone, cloth and paper. To stories we can touch. We yearn and thirst for what is real, what was born in the ancient earth.

***

Consider the book and the magazine and the newspaper as technology. They have myriad access points. They are portable. They require no plug nor battery. They can be consumed while supine or in a sampan or at sea. They are recyclable. They can be consumed repeatedly and in some cases should be. They can be operated by infants or elders. They are not draped by safety strictures. They pass easily into hundreds of languages. They are blessedly silent in a world of wheedling. They are designed for your hands. Most of them are substantial in a world of illusion. They can last thousands of years. They are envelopes for ideas. They are objects of grace and beauty. They are envelopes for epiphanies. They harbor hope. They have heft. They wait for you to find them. They grow battered and beloved. Even when ancient they are filled with verve and brio. They preserve voices. They are immortal. They are extraordinary. We take them for granted. Perhaps that is what we do with what we love.

***

If the only way we ever are informed and stimulated and moved and edified and educated and enlightened and electrified is through electronic means, are we customers or captives?

# A NOTE ON PORNOGRAPHY

You know what nobody ever talks about enough when we talk about pornography? How sad it is. How sad everything about it is. How weary and dreary. How draining and unfruitful. How, simply, *embarrassing*. How deflating and abasing. How melancholy and grim. How sad the users and purchasers are, and how ashamed of themselves for using and purchasing and hiding what they have used and purchased; how sad the purveyors are, and how ashamed of themselves for manufacturing a product that has no substance, and how weary they are, deep in their hearts, of the tinny shrill language they use to defend their actions, for they know full well that their actions have nothing to do with free speech, with courage against the tyranny of censorship, with salty rebellion against those who would imprison speech as a crucial step to the murder of dissent. They know that they prey on sadness for money, prey on the sad women and men who perform the empty rituals, the sad men and women who run the cameras and produce and package and market the brittle shells of acts that are, when not sad, funny and powerful and glorious and moving and extraordinary, acts ancient beyond our calculation, acts without which there would be no human beings at all, acts that are holy, acts that are finally a form of dance, of speech, of prayer.

And another thing we don't talk about when we talk about pornography is that there are lots of kinds of pornography, if you consider pornography to be the shell masquerading as the substance. A politician shouting endlessly about family values and yet doing everything in his power to battle help for single mothers, and suspend education for poor children, and dispute free food for those who are starving, and oppose medical care for those who have none — isn't he a pornographer? Or the woman who battles the execution of infants (for that is what abortion is) but advocates executing older infants (for that is what capital punishment is) — isn't she a pornographer too? Or the men who spend thousands of hours working for the right to marry each other, and no hours working for the children who are murdered on their street, their city, their state, their country — aren't they pornographers? Isn't it obscene to say that love is the prime force, and then argue about semantics and definitions so that children may be slurped from wombs and quietly disposed of in biohazard containers?

And even the church, my church, that ancient and wonderful boat, the church I love and respect and admire, the church that has thrilled me with its courage and stunned me with its twisted crimes — does it not dabble in pornography daily? Does it not say one thing and do another? Does it not say that life is the most precious and holy of gifts from the Unimaginable One, and then send armies of theologians to defend the unutterably obscene idea of a just war? For there is no such thing as a just war, as you know and I know deep in our hearts. Wars are merely organized murders, during which lanky children die and everyone else rationalizes the reasons. So if we know a thing to be true — that life is holy, for example, and life cannot be taken for any reason whatsoever, and the taking of a life, new or old, is a sin — and then we create tissues and curtains of excuses and lies to cover our knowledge, are we much different from the polite dapper businessman who runs a company selling images of people making love, though there is no love anywhere to be found in the product that he sells?

We have tried to restrict and imprison pornography for centuries, and now it is more popular than ever before; it has burst out everywhere, on billboards and films, on a million web sites, in every city on the face of the earth. But I wonder if the way to defeat pornography is to see that it is a symptom, not the disease. Lust is sweet and holy and wild, lust is who we are, lust is a gift. The perversion of lust, however — that is the spawn of a cultural and religious lie of breathtaking proportions. It is a lie so huge that we can hardly see it. But for a moment, today, this morning, let us stop and see it clearly.

As a culture, as a religion, we say one thing and do another, and we have become so used to living this way that substance and appearance are in danger of becoming the same thing.

That would be a very good definition of hell, don't you think?

# IRRECONCILABLE DISSONANCE

I have been married once, so far, to the woman to whom I am still married, so far, and one thing I have noticed about being married, so far, is that it makes you a lot more attentive to divorce, which used to seem like something that happened to other people but doesn't any more, because of course every marriage is pregnant with divorce, and now I know a lot of people who are divorced, or about to be, or somewhere in between those poles, for which shadowy status there should be words like *mivorced* or *darried* or *sleeperated* or *schleperated,* but there aren't, so far.

People get divorced for all sorts of reasons, and I find myself taking notes, probably defensively, but also from sheer amazement at the chaotic wilderness of human nature. For example, I read recently about one man who got divorced so he could watch all sixty episodes of *The Wire* in chronological order. Another man got divorced after thirty years so he could, he said, fart in peace. Another man got divorced in part because he told his wife he had an affair but he *didn't* have an affair, he just couldn't think of any other good excuse to get divorced, and he didn't *want* to have an affair, or be with anyone else other than his wife, he *liked* his wife, and rather enjoyed her company as a rule, he said, but he just didn't want to be married to her *every* day anymore, he preferred to be married to her every third day, maybe, but she did not find that a workable arrangement, and so they parted company, confused.

Another man I read about didn't want to get divorced, he said, but when his wife kept insisting that they get divorced because she had fallen in love with another guy, he, the husband, finally agreed to get divorced, and soon after he found himself dating the other guy's first wife, which, as the first guy said, who could invent such a story? The other guy soon dumped the first guy's wife, which made the husband feel terrible for his former wife, but by then the train was long gone from the station, he said.

I read about a woman who divorced her husband because he picked his nose. I read about a woman who got divorced because her husband never remembered to pay their property taxes and finally, she said, it was just too much. Is it so very much to ask, she asked, that the person who shares responsibility for your life remembers to pay the taxes? Does this have to be a crisis every year? She seemed sort of embarrassed to say what she said but she said it.

It seems to me that the reasons people divorce are hardly ever the dramatic reasons we assume are the reasons people get divorced, like sex in motels and cocaine for breakfast and discovering that the guy you married ten years ago has a wife in Wisconsin. It's more a quiet decay, it seems, as if marriages are houses and unless you keep cleaning the windows and repainting here and there and using duct tape with deft punctilio, after a while everything sags and mold wins and there you are signing settlement papers at the dining room table.

I read about a couple who got divorced because of *irresolute differences,* a phrase that addled me for weeks. Another couple filed for divorce on the grounds of *irreconcilable dissonance,* which seemed like one of those few cases in life when the exact right words are applied to the exact right reason for those words. I read about another woman who divorced her husband because one time they were walking down the street, the husband on the curb side in concordance with the ancient courteous male custom of being on that side so as to receive the splatter of mud or worse from the street and keep such splatter from the pristine acreage of his beloved, and as they approached a fire hydrant he lifted his leg, puppylike, as a joke, and the wife marched right to a lawyer's office and instituted divorce proceedings. That particular woman refused to speak to reporters about the reasons for divorce but you wonder what the iceberg was under *that* surface, you know?

The first divorce I saw up close, like the first car crash you see up close, is imprinted on the inside of my eyelids, and I still think about it, not because it happened, but because years after it happened it seems so fated to have happened. How could it be that a couple who really liked each other, and took the brave crazy flyer on not just living together, which lots of mammals do, but swearing fealty and respect in front of a huge crowd, and filing taxes as a joint entity, and spawning a child, and co-signing mortgages and car loans, how could they end up signing settlement papers on the dining room table, and weeping in the garden, and being coldly polite to each other at the door when he comes to pick up the kid on Saturday? How could that be?

The saddest word I've heard wrapped around divorce like a tattered blanket is *tired*, as in *we were just both tired*, because tired seems so utterly normal to me, so much the rug always bunching in that one spot no matter what you do, the slightly worn dish rack, the belt with extra holes punched with an ice pick that you borrowed from your cousin for exactly this purpose, the flashlight in the pantry which has never had batteries and never will, that the thought of *tired* being both your daily bread and also grounds for divorce gives me the willies. The shagginess of things, the way they never quite work out as planned and break down every other Tuesday, necessitating wine and foul language and duct tape and the wrong-sized screw quietly hammered into place with the bottom of the garden gnome, seems to me the very essence of marriage; so if what makes a marriage work – the constant shifting of expectations and eternal parade of small surprises – is also what causes marriages to dissolve, where is it safe to stand?

Nowhere, of course. Every marriage is pregnant with divorce, every day, every hour, every minute. The second you finish reading this essay, your spouse could close the refrigerator, after miraculously finding a way to wedge the juice carton behind the milk jug, and call your marriage quits, and the odd truth of the matter is that because he or she might end your marriage in a moment, and you might end his or hers, you're still married. The instant there is no chance of death is the moment of death.

# THE TERRIBLE BRILLIANCE

I'll tell you a story. My wife is an art teacher for kids who are really really sick, a job filled with hilarity and pain, a job she loves, a job that makes her shiver and go for long walks in the hills. She spent a lot of time recently doing art projects with a girl who got sicker and sicker and endured oceans of pain and grew more swollen and weary by the day, and one day I came home to find my wife sad to the bottom of her bones. I asked her what was the matter and she said some things that haunt me still, and I think you should hear them.

She's being crucified, said my wife. Everything they do to her hurts. All those needles are nails. All the mothers watching and wincing and weeping in the shower later. All the little crucifixions. She just accepts it. She never complains. She gets crucified every day. All the little children being crucified. Why does this happen? Why does this happen?

There was nothing to say, of course, so I didn't say anything, and the next day she went back up to the hospital and did art projects with kids who are really really sick.

You know what we never talk about when we talk about our faith? The awful genius of it, the horrific honesty. We say that Christ died for us because we need some terrible inarticulate way to hold death quivering in our hearts. We need some way to pray for that girl and all the kids like her and the only way that makes any sense is the nonsensical, illogical, unreasonable, insupportable, unprovable conviction that one time long time ago a thin young mysterious eloquent Jewish guy was crucified and died and then he came alive again in a way that no one understood then and no one understands now. If that happened, then there is a way for us to live amid the sea of death; if that didn't happen we are only compost, awake for a time and then put to work as seething soil.

I am not talking theological babble or pontifical edict or

regulatory murk. I am talking about the haunting human genius in the marrow of Catholicism. A mother watched her son be tortured and crucified and she held him in her arms and there are no words for what she felt. A mother watched her daughter be tortured and crucified and she held her in her arms and there are no words for what she felt. It happens all day every day everywhere. All the little crucifixions. All the tiny Christs. The terrible brilliance of our faith is that there isn't one Christ, there are billions, and each one suffers for and saves the rest, in ways that we will never understand. All we can do is tiptoe into a kid's room, and spread out all the holy colors on her bed, and make her laugh, and witness her pain and courage, and sing her grace under duress. Somehow she will come alive again, and there will be a light on her mother's face for which there are no words, and all the things we ever said about what we believe will turn out to be true. That will be a good day. That will be the best day ever.

# ONE NIGHT

The coolest story about the Catholic university where I work is that there isn't one – there are zillions, some of which are hilarious, like the gentlemanly land scam idea the founders had for paying for the new place, or the time the university president traded the bull that serviced local cows for a new car, and some are haunting, like the time a university president had a heart attack and died on a stage right after saying farewell to the assemblage, or the boy ninety years ago who moved into his dorm room and then dove in the river and never came back up again, and some are hilarious but tense, like a new vice president forty years ago discovering that the university was technically bankrupt and his first official phone call was begging and wheedling to the bank, and some are sweet and nutty, like the way the university's women's soccer team used to wander up into the stands barefoot after a game to shake hands with every kid who wanted to shake hands and get autographs, and then there are some stories that make you shiver and pray.

Like this one.

Recently I sat in a little chapel filled with one hundred boys upon whom unimaginable crimes and sins had been committed, boys who had endured and survived more species of pain and desolation than I could account in a year, boys who had been married to sadness for years, boys who were thrashing all day every day toward some kind of shivering peace and rebirth, and every one of these boys was bouncing his feet, or nodding his head, or grinning widely, or snapping his fingers, because there was a university alumnus standing where the altar usually is, and he was singing and roaring, and banging away beautifully on his enormous guitar, and the wild deft musicians behind him were making a muscle of music so joyous and fast and captivating that you just could *not* sit still, no matter how cool you wanted to seem, or how deep inside yourself you crouched as protection against rage and pain and fire, and the boy in front of me was rocking and bouncing like he was about to launch into space, and then he burst into tears, and he cried for the rest of the hour, although he never stopped rocking and bouncing for an instant. I watched his tears slide down his face into his suit jacket, which was hairy and too small for him, and I wondered how many tears had been wept into that jacket, but there is no way to tell.

At the end of the concert, when the band had finished with an incredible flourish and it was okay for everyone to jump up and yell, the boy shot out of his chair and jumped up and down laughing until finally he and everyone else settled down to a dull roar and began to file out of the pews. Then every single boy in the chapel went up to the members of the band and shook their hands and said thank you, sir, and then they lined up in barrack order and walked out of the chapel rustling and humming.

I saw this. I was there. I'll never forget that boy. Something hit his heart right amidships, right in the place where joy and hope were down to their last lost grains, and it was a man from and of and about this university who delivered that thrilling blow, and I saw it delivered, and I saw it land. That's what universities are for, hitting kids in the heart. It happens all the time. It happens in a zillion ways. I saw one way, one night, and I'll never forget it.

# THE ORDER IN WHICH
# PEOPLE ARE ADMITTED TO HEAVEN

To be admitted without review by committee: children under the age of twelve, sixth-grade teachers, the mothers of triplets, janitors, nuns (all religions), nurses, all other mothers, loggers, policemen with more than ten years of service, Buddhists (see Appendix A), bass players in rock bands, librettists, gardeners, cartographers, eighth-grade teachers, cellists, farriers, veterinarians, magicians, compass-makers, firemen and firewomen, rare-book-room librarians, cobblers, anyone from the former Gilbert Islands in the South Pacific, breakfast cooks in diners, philologists, proofreaders, administrative assistants and secretaries, sauciers, mapmakers, cartwrights, cartoonists, essayists, people who manufacture thimbles, and Presbyterians (see Appendix B).

To be admitted after cursory review by committee: archeologists, Catholics, Jews, Muslims, Hindus, B'hais, doctors (except orthodontists; see Appendix C), plumbers, taxi-drivers, boatwrights, soldiers actually engaged in defending their clan or country from attack or threatened attack, undertakers, popes without children, longshoremen, tugboat pilots, coaches of any elementary-school sport whatsoever (precedence for basketball and Australian Rules football coaches), all other teachers, cellists, anyone who ever worked on an auction for a nonprofit, scuba-divers, publishers of children's books, people from Finland, people who sell life insurance (it turns out life insurance is something really really close to the Director's heart), anyone who ever took a tango lesson, hotel doormen, people who brew beer in their bathtubs, child-care-center directors, emergency dispatchers, detectives, monks, anyone in the peanut-butter industry, paddle-surfers (female), bus drivers, fishmongers, anyone who ever repaired a copy machine or a child's bicycle, and any father who ever wiped or bathed a child other than his own without complaint.

To be admitted under the special Mother of the Lord provision ("the back door"): Unitarians, Pete Maravich, exotic dancers, journalists (see Appendix D).

To be admitted under the special Saint Joseph provision ("the Wauvoo door"): male paddle-surfers, Sir Donald Bradman, muleskinners, a man named Wemera who lived ten thousand years ago in what is today Brazil, highway construction and repair crews, and Mormons (see Appendix E).

To be admitted only by special appeal to the Director: theatrical agents, bishops, anyone who ever sold marijuana or alcohol to a child, avant-garde artists, mimes, Senators, Caesars, pharaohs, preachers, short-story writers (Flannery O'Connor excepted), and any leader of a state who has called himself, or instructed others to call him, The Great Helmsman, The Dear Leader, President for Life, Brother Leader, Father of the Country, etc.

To be admitted only after review by the Screening Board (Catherine of Siena, chairwoman), the Board of Appeals (Meher Baba, chairman), and the Last Gasp Committee (Joseph Cardinal Bernardin, chairman): poets, novelists, buskers, spies, New York Yankee fans.

To be admitted if Hell freezes over: flautists, ethicists, sommeliers, magazine editors, Iosif Vissarionovich Dzhugashvili (also known as Joseph Stalin), and Mao Zedong. There are any number of other names on this list; two per year rotate to the top for public promulgation, as here. The other names are held in the heart of the Director. Believe me it isn't worth asking Him about the other names. We have tried and tried, and have invented sly angles for asking the question, like "Your Lovingness, sir, can Hitler be forgiven and admitted into the Ocean of Joy, and now what's the story with Osama bin Muhammad bin Awad bin Ladin, is he sentenced to an eternity of preening for a shoddy video production as he did in life but this time the camera never works no matter how much he yells at his flunkies?" But He just smiles, you know how He does that, it drives you nuts, that smile, talk about your mysterious gnomic grins, but what can you do, you know what I mean?

---

APPENDIX A: Those to whom all life is holy, and who act in accordance to this belief, have worn the seamless garment, and are admitted without qualification, no matter what religion they professed, or lack thereof.

APPENDIX B: Robert Louis Stevenson was a Presbyterian, so all Presbyterians before and after his tenure on earth (1850-1894) are admitted, by direct fiat of the Director.

APPENDIX C: This class of men and women is under review. For 2011 they are classed with cosmetic surgeons, psychics, and the owners of psychedelia shops as probationary.

APPENDIX D: Unitarians, bless their earnest hearts, are admitted without further ado, but the debate over the qualifications of journalists as a class go back millennia and have generated many planets' worth of legal records. For the year 2011 print and radio journalists are given precedence over web journalists. Television journalists are, as usual, not admitted but this year for the first time are allowed to file appeals with Mr. Edward Murrow.

APPENDIX E: The ways and means of the Director are fascinating and often beyond the ken of the recording secretary. Wemera is said to be the most compassionate man who ever lived, at least according to pub talk up here; details are filed in the Library. Sir Donald Bradman, an Australian of the twentieth century after the birth of the Son of Light, was the greatest cricket player who ever lived, and you know how the Director feels about cricket. As regards the Mormons, which is what they are called here, although they much prefer to be called members of the church of Jesus Christ of Latter-Day Saints, they have been, since the year 1912 after the Incarnation, admitted without further ado if they can be made to giggle at the idea of Joseph Smith staring into his hat and reading there the burning words of the new book of holies, but hey, Catholicism, to pick another human religious path, has its own weird adventures, like people praying over the shards of the sternums of saints, and seeing the Madonna on tortillas and cinnamon rolls and stop- signs, and making like my boy Joseph of Cupertino and suddenly leaping into the air and floating there for a while, which he liked to do here in his first few weeks, but then he realized that everyone here leaps and floats, because we are in the presence of the Director, who is Joy incarnate. But you knew that.

# HIS FATHER

Well, here's a story I never told before, but it's been haunting me, so I think I have to tell it, because I'm pretty sure no one else will, and if a story doesn't get told, isn't that a door that never gets a chance to open, and isn't that a shame and a sin?

So then.

I was in college. This was in the middle of America thirty years ago. It was the last night I was ever in college. There was a huge roaring tumultuous party in our hall. It was a very old hall with ironwork everywhere and vaulted ceilings and all the students who were not graduating yet had gone home so our hall echoed with music and shouting and laughter and chaos and merriment. Of course almost every student who was about to graduate had family members arriving for the weekend, so a few sisters and brothers and even a dad or two joined the party, and everyone tried to chat up the new girls, and then people from other halls who heard the roar from our hall wandered over, and soon it was midnight and the party was throbbing and even the shyest people were dancing and giggling and shouting.

It was a really great party.

At about one in the morning I noticed that the dad of a friend of mine was in the corner drinking hard and telling funny stories. He got drunker and drunker until at about three in the morning he started shouting and cursing and some glass smashed and finally he fell down. Seeing a dad huddled in a moist heap on our linoleum floor was a great shock. I had never seen a drunken dad before. My dad liked to tell of the three times he had been drunk in his whole life, once in the war and one time with the neighbors and one time in the city, but my brothers and I thought he was probably exaggerating to prove that he was like other dads, which he wasn't.

At the party that night my friend picked up his crumpled dad, and held him in his arms like a fireman holding a child, and slid grimly along the wall to the door, and propped the door open with his foot, and carried his dad outside. I watched him do this but did nothing to help. I just stood there. Not the first time and not the last that I would stand silent and useless and frozen.

Over the next thirty years I never said a word about that night and neither did my friend. Here and there he would leak a story about a moment when he was a kid and his dad was carried home by the police, or about getting his dad out of the drunk tank, or about the morning his mom changed the locks on their house, or about how his sister went to live with their dad but came home grim a day later, or about how one of the brothers died in a car crash and the father didn't make the funeral, or about how when the dad died finally they put his ashes in a whiskey bottle, but we never talked about that night at the party. All the rest of my life I'll remember my friend's face as he carried his father in his arms that night, though. I'll never forget that. You think we have words for this sort of thing but we do not. All we can do is witness and report and hope that somehow stories turn into prayers. All we can do is drape words on experience, and hope the words give some hint of the shape of the moment, and pray that our attentiveness matters in a way we will never know. I believe, with all my heart, that it does. What do you believe?

# III.

# LET IT GO

Here's a story. Two years ago I sat at the end of my bed at three in the morning, in tears, furious, frightened, exhausted, as drained and hopeless as I have ever been in this bruised and blessed world, at the very end of the end of my rope, and She spoke to me. I know it was Her. I have no words with which to tell you how sure I am that it was the Mother. Trust me.

*Let it go,* She said.

The words were clear, unambiguous, crisp, unadorned. They appeared whole and gentle and adamant in my mind, more clearly than if they had somehow been spoken in the dark salt of the room. I have never had words delivered to me so clearly and powerfully and yet so gently and patiently, never.

*Let it go.*

I did all the things you would do in that situation. I sat bolt upright. I looked around me. I listened for more words. I looked out the window to see if someone was standing in the garden talking to me through the window. I wondered for a second if my wife or children had spoken in their sleep. I waited for Her to say something more. She didn't speak again. The words hung sizzling in my mind for a long time and then faded. It's hard to explain. It's like they were lit and then the power slowly ebbed.

*Let it go.*

She knew how close I was to absolute utter despair, to a sort of madness, to a country in which many sweet and holy things would be broken, and She reached for me and cupped me in Her hand and spoke into the me of me and I will never forget Her voice until the day I die. I think about it every day. I hold those words close and turn them over and over and look at them in every light and from every angle.

For more than a year I told no one about this, not even my wife whom I love dearly and who has a heart bigger than a star, but then

I told two friends, and I told them because they told me that they too had been Spoken to in moments of great darkness. A clan of the consoled, and there must be millions of us.

Billions.

We say a great deal about the Mother. We speak of her in Mass, in schools, in magazines and newspapers and newsletters and bulletins, in seminaries and schools, in colleges and on web sites, and we know nothing of Whom we speak. All we know is a handful of stories from two thousand years ago, shreds and shards, tattered threads from what must have been even then an unimaginable fabric. Miriam, she was named, מרים in the Hebrew, and She lived, married, Bore Him, endured, wept over His icy corpse, died. When She died Her body rose into the heavens and vanished from earthly view.

But I tell you that She spoke to me one cold wet night in western Oregon and Her words are burned on my heart as if She reached down with a finger like a sweet razor and traced them there at three in the morning and I cannot explain how Her words changed everything and how there was the first part of my life and now there is the part after She spoke to me.

*Let it go.*

I still have a job and kids and my mysterious wife and a bad back and a nasal mutter and too many bills, nothing's changed outwardly, I didn't drop everything and hit the road hunched over in mooing prayer and song, and there are still all sorts of things quietly muddled and loudly screeching in my life, but something astonishing happened to me two years ago and it changed everything. Something broke and something healed, something so deep and joyous that I cannot find words for it, hard as I try.

We say a great deal about the Mother and we know nothing of Whom we speak. That is what I want to say to you. But She knows us. Trust me when I say that I know this to be true. Whatever else you hear today, whatever else you read, whatever else happens in your life, whatever way your heart is bruised and elevated today, remember that.

# LITANY OF THE BLESSED MOTHER

Mother most exasperated but calm in the face of total sneering and whining from her progeny whom she loves although sometimes she would like to upend them face first in the laundry bin which is crammed with their clothes *anyways*, pray for us.

Mother most unable to find even four minutes by herself to sit calmly in the locked bathroom and try to breathe slowly so as not to pop a gasket because as soon as any child senses that she is not available for instant cheerful maid-and-kitchen service comes a banging on the door and wailing most piteously, pray for us.

Mother who set the all-time world and Olympic record for kneeling not in prayer but to mop the kitchen floor and the bedroom floor where someone got sick and the bathroom floor covered with wet towels and clumps and hair and shreds of tissue and apple juice where someone wasn't supposed to bring it in the bathroom when bathing for exactly this reason, pray for us.

Queen of the used-car lot and rummage sale and farmer's market and second-day bread store and auction and bruised-produce bin and sub-prime-mortgage-offer-seemingly-too-good-to-refuse who now weeps silently at three in the morning after assuring her weary and grim husband that they will work it out no problem no worries, pray for us.

Mostly patient ear for the grumbles and snarls and snores and testiness and greediness and selfishness and mutters and sarcasms and smelly shoes of her husband whom she does love all the time in a deep way hard to explain even to herself and does like about every other day or so even when he is being an utter bonehead which he is enough that twice a week she thinks quickly and guiltily perhaps she *should* have married the guy who sang tenor in the church choir, pray for us.

Ark of all information about insurance forms and car registrations and school fees and computer passwords and tax codes and phone numbers for plumbers and hours that the library is open on Sunday if it is open at all which seems to be for some reason a source of weekly debate, pray for us.

Tower of virtue except for the very slight daydreaming she does about the older man at the coffee shop who looks so dignified and urbane with his superb Italian shoes and his handsome calm dog and his lovely long clean car and his apparently unmarried or formerly married existence and the way his hair has just begun to go silver at his lean elegant temples in the most attractive way not that she ever would ever do anything or even speak to him but there's no harm in daydreaming a little and in fact it's healthy, isn't it, pray for us.

Vessel of honor who *did* report a minor cheating incident committed by a minor female citizen to the principal of the middle school and also to the pastor much to the shrieking weeping recriminations and insults of the minor in question who is still bitter about it and may never in this lifetime forgive this act although I hope to God she someday understands that perhaps this small public embarrassment helped build a lifelong sense of honesty and integrity but who am I kidding will be the villain of this piece until kingdom come, pray for us.

Mystical rose who often thinks that if not for daily plunges into her wild seething vigorous redolent garden and the dense moist nearby woods and the occasional long solitary wander along the shore of the lake at dawn she would go stark raving muttering gibbering insane from the press of tinny plastic shrill empty shallow greedy Modernity, pray for us.

Comforter of friends who are being divorced and who are divorcing, comforter of those imprisoned in icy wards of hospitals where one or more breasts will be removed, comforter of those who receive their Meals on Wheels with ill grace, comforter of priests who suddenly weep at lunch and confess that they are lonely lonely lonely and miss more than anything the hugs of children which are now forbidden and will never come again, pray for us.

Mother who endured the unendurable, mother who holds and salves and saves us, mother to whom we whisper in the blue hours of the night, mother whose gentle smile is our food, mother without whom we would die of despair, mother to whom we will run sobbing and laughing when our chapter closes and the path to your arms opens wide,

Pray for us, pray for us, pray for us,

Amen.

# A NOTE ON SECRETS

I'll tell you a secret. One time I made out with a girl in a bus as her best friend, my date, smoking a cigarette, waited for us outside the bus, and when I got off the bus my date took one look at my face and tried to put her cigarette out in my eye. I don't know how she knew what had to be the shortest-lived secret ever and still don't know. She never spoke to me again, and neither did her friend.

This was not the first time women and secrets led me to murky confusion, where I have lived ever since. The first girl I ever kissed swore me to secrecy, but we were fourteen years old then and I didn't actually have anyone to tell the secret to, since my brothers and friends would have fallen down laughing at the very idea that a girl had kissed *me*, and besides the whole actual kissing event was a muddle: I had major spectacles and she had complicated braces and neither of us knew how to breathe while kissing (did you come up for air every thirty seconds like swimming, or take turns breathing, or breathe like walruses through your noses or what) and our shy clinking kisses, in a dank dark basement with peeling paneling and moaning music and moist potato chips in a sad chipped bowl, were more like spaceships docking in the vast silence of deep space than they were heated or romantic or anything like that and anyway our few tentative kisses were ended abruptly by her roaring father who was supposed to be elsewhere but suddenly and definitively wasn't.

After that it seemed that every girl I met was webbed with secrets, and whenever a girl told me a secret, or we did something that was supposed to be secret, soon there were bad plot devices and furious friends and car keys thrown in creeks and I was an idiot. This happened all the time, even with my cool sister, who liked to smoke and swore me to secrecy and soon there were various smoking implements and implications on the kitchen table and our dad simmering and somehow this was all my fault and my sister threatened to snap my pinkies like twigs but thankfully she didn't, or hasn't yet.

As I got older the secrets got harder. By the time I was thirty I had been told heartbreaking secrets – about rapes and abortions and arrests and addictions and betrayals on a dizzying scale – and I grew seared and salted and seasoned by them, forced to understand that *everyone* has wounds and burdens and scars slashed on their hearts; and it turns out the most amazing thing about our species isn't that we all have secret pains but that everyone carries their loads with such grace and endurance. *That's* astonishing. Not a day goes by, not an hour, when I am not knocked out by grace under duress, the greatest secret of all.

Now I am fifty, older than dirt, with children who are sure I voted for Lincoln for president, but I am still nailed by secrets, all of them starting with the same six chilling words, *I have something to tell you,* the words that flank secrets like cops around a motorcade; and the secrets are more unbearable than ever: wars hatched by lies, children raped by priests, wives who stare out the window at the rain as their husbands make love to them. And more than ever I am absorbed by women and their secrets, though I no longer find cigarettes aimed at my eye; my mom, for example, a riveting woman with a thousand tales to tell, recently told me that I had two brothers I never knew, each dying after mere minutes in this world, which makes *three* brothers I never knew, my brother Seamus dying suddenly when he was five months old, a secret I discovered when I was fifteen years old and found a book of photographs one day in the attic and wondered who the baby was and when I showed the book to my mom her face fell in a way that I still all these years later cannot explain very well.

My daughter just turned fifteen years old and she is an ocean of secrets and sometimes I stand in the kitchen ostensibly doing the dishes but really thinking about all the things I don't know about her and never will know. I used to know everything about her, every flicker of her face, every note of every sound that issued from the bud of her lips; I rocked her and bathed her and heard her first words and saw her first staggering steps and wept when she went to kindergarten that first day with her bright dress and brighter smile, and now she is all willowy and sneery and womanish and I don't know anything at all really about what she does all day and late into the night except what she tells me, which is not much, and what her mother tells me, which is a secret, so after nearly four decades of careful study I am more muddled by women than ever before, which sometimes seems like a roaring accomplishment to me, on the theory that whenever you are sure about anything, you are certainly wrong, isn't that so?

# SIX WOMEN

A while ago I met a renowned priest, a man nationally respected for his work in higher education. He was about sixty then, this fellow, quiet, witty, shy. A very accomplished man. He told me many things but the most interesting thing was that he said he had learned more about holiness from the six women he had dated before he became a priest than from anyone else, an assertion I found riveting, so I asked him to talk about those six women, which he did with refreshing honesty and eloquence.

My first girlfriend, he said, taught me to pay attention, to listen, to get past the fact that she was beautiful and alluring and get down to the real person under that remarkably attractive surface. In the end she fell in love with another man. So she taught me about pain and loss, too - but those are the coins of this realm.

I remember her with affection, he said.

My next girlfriend, he continued, was eloquent and articulate and *very* funny. To be with her was to have your life italicized, know what I mean? Every moment was exciting and vigorous. She taught me about living more intently, about joy, about energy and creativity and seizing the moment. And she taught me about loss, too, in a different way - she said to me one day, gently, that we just drove at different speeds in life, and she could tell that this would grind on us and make us bitter over the years, and we should have the courage now to stop, that honesty is an act of love too even when it is freighted with sadness, which is true.

Then I dated a family friend, he said, and that was sweet and warm, but I found after a while that I didn't feel for her what she felt for me, and so we moved along, and then I dated a woman who was a glorious dancer, and I liked the way she forced me to attend to the holiness of physicality, you know? We danced and climbed mountains and ran road races and that sort of thing, and while we weren't compatible enough in other areas to go deeper with each other, she taught me to savor the world and how everything that lives and moves is really a prayer of celebration.

Then I met a woman, he said, with whom I was crazy in love, and we planned to marry. But there came a night I had to tell her that something was still gnawing at me way deep in my soul, and I just had to chase after that, it wouldn't be honest for her or me if I didn't, and that was hard. That was when I first knew, I think, that I couldn't get away from the idea of being a priest. I lay awake that night, I can tell you, thinking I had ruined my life and hers. I quit my job then, and quit that love affair, and went back to school, where I later met a woman who became my best friend, and being in love with her taught me finally that the deepest love is the deepest friendship, that attraction and compatibility and all are great and necessary in dense and honest relationships, but the deepest bone is absolute care about the other person's heart, the sort of feeling that really *is* why you would give up your life without a second thought for someone you love, that's how soldiers feel about their comrades and how parents feel about their kids and how thousands of men and women I have met feel about their spouses and lovers, which is, when you think about it collectively, an occasion of overwhelming joy, that we are capable of such selfless love, don't you think?

And finally, he said, being in love with her was how I realized that for me Christ was my deepest friend, and I was going to be a priest. It was a joyous realization, very peaceful, like coming home from a very long journey. And my best friend was thrilled for me, because she loved me, and wanted me to be the best and truest and happiest man I could be. We are dear friends still, all these years later, and always will be, I hope and pray.

The best preparation for me as a priest, he said, was to love women, haltingly and poorly and then more honestly and deeply, until finally I married the wild idea that God is love and love defeats death and we will live forever in the unimaginable love of Christ. I love being a priest. It's what I was made for. But I would have never seen my path clear to God without those six women.

He said this with a gentle smile I'll always remember.

Me, personally, after listening to this extraordinary priest, I wondered how many other priests would say something similar. I wondered if maybe a better way to prepare priests is to raise the age limit and accept only men who have loved and lost and loved again. I wondered if anyone in our blessed and blinkered church has ever stated bluntly that learning to love women is crucial to being a man. We don't say that much. We should. We would have a far healthier church if we were far more honest about love in all its wild and confusing forms – all of which are, in the end, God, yes?

# THAT'S JUST HOW HE WAS

Saw a man die yesterday. He was an old man, sitting in a folding chair, and he leaned his head back and closed his eyes and died. His name was Leonard. He was a veteran of the Second World War. He was sitting with other veterans of the war under a big white tent at a memorial for men and women who died in that particular war.

One war among many.

It was raining. A speaker was speaking about courage.

After a couple of minutes the man next to Leonard asked if he was okay and when Leonard didn't say anything the man touched him on the shoulder and Leonard slumped over a little and then there was a ruckus.

Some men carried Leonard over to a big cedar tree and under the tree an old priest knelt in the redolent fallen needles and blessed Leonard's soul as it flew away. The old priest had been in the Army too. Another priest led a prayer and everyone who was there said *amen* as if they had never said the word before.

Then some men carried Leonard into a building nearby and they placed him gently on the floor and set up folding chairs in a circle around him and Leonard's wife and children sat with him for a long time as policewomen and firemen and medics and such came and went. They hugged each other, the family did, and they cried a little, but mostly they sat and prayed quietly.

Outside the building the memorial service for men and women who fought in wars went on. The rain fell gently.

Inside the building the family held hands and waited. A tall girl brought sandwiches and coffee for the family. No one said much. The family ate quietly. The memorial service concluded with measured gunfire and a lonely trumpet.

My grandpa, he loved to talk, said Leonard's granddaughter. He would talk to *anyone*. And he sure could listen. He was a great listener. He was very opinionated. He was a firm-minded man. He would give you the shirt off his back. He loved the blackest thickest coffee possible. He had been a brakeman and a conductor on the railroad. He sure liked to watch the news on television. He liked travel shows also. He was a sergeant in the war. He never said much about the war. He loved to make pies. He loved gospel music. He loved to make chili also. He read the Bible every day. He was the most jovial and affable and gregarious man you ever saw. Everyone had a good word for him and he had a good word for everyone. That's just how he was. Wherever he went everyone would turn toward him with a smile and a good word. That's just how he was.

Finally some men carried Leonard away and his family walked to their cars and drove home.

I watched Leonard's wife drive away, her passenger seat empty, and thought many thoughts: of her empty hours to come, of her lonely bed, of her calm in the face of death, of the inexplicable holy shape of her love for him and his love for her, of her courage, of the way her hand opened time after time to accept the sorrowful hands of others; just as hearts open to accept hearts.

# GOING TO JAIL

You enter through a door in the back where a big sign says **ALL PRISONERS MUST BE SHACKLED**. Prisoners who have never been to the jail generally go to the front door and press the bell and are told by the crackling intercom to go around the back which they do. To get to the back door you walk through the parking lot where there are cop cars and tow trucks. At the back door you wait with the other prisoners.

New prisoners are admitted at seven in the evening.

There are seven men waiting by the door tonight. Five are white and two are brown. The youngest might be twenty years old and the oldest might be sixty. Four men have plastic grocery bags with their personal effects and one man has a brown paper bag with his personal effects and another man cradles his personal effects in his arms and the youngest man has no personal effects that I can see.

One man waits by the door for a moment and then strolls over to a car across the street. There is a woman in the car, in the driver's seat, and he says something to her but she doesn't look at him or speak to him. The man opens the back door of the car and snaps his fingers and a dog jumps out and nuzzles his hand and the dog and the man walk off around the block, the man lighting a cigarette as he goes.

One of the men by the back door of the jail is standing with a woman and two small boys. The man and the woman and the boys all have short blonde hair. The woman is talking quietly to the man. The boys are maybe six and four years old and they are running around and knocking each other down and bickering and laughing and whining. The younger boy tries to spit on his brother but he misses. The woman says something terse and firm to the boys and for a half-second they settle down but soon they are crashing around again.

The blonde man watches them but he doesn't say anything.

The man with the personal effects cradled in his arms is surrounded by a knot of friends who are not going to jail this evening. The friends are all joking and laughing and the man going to jail banters a little too but then he falls silent.

After a while a police officer shows up with a roster of the prisoners who are to be admitted this evening. He reads off the names one by one and as he reads your name you line up by the door. When he has read the names of six of the men he prepares to open the door, but the seventh man, the man who looks like he might be twenty, says to him, My name is Moreno.

I beg your pardon? says the policeman.

Moreno.

Sir, I don't have you on the admitting list.

I must be here seven o'clock.

Moreno?

Moreno. I have a letter.

May I see the letter?

I don't have the letter now. Moreno. Seven o'clock.

The policeman talks to the intercom for a moment and then he turns back to the young man and says, Well, we don't have you on the admitting list for tonight, sir, but come on in and we will square this away, okay?

Okay, says Moreno.

You have any personal effects, Mr. Moreno?

No sir.

Okay then. Come on in.

The door opens and the men walk in single file under the sign that says **ALL PRISONERS MUST BE SHACKLED**. Three of the men with personal effects in plastic bags go first, and then the man who had been walking the dog and smoking, and then the man with his personal effects in his arms, and then the blonde man, who kneels down for a moment to hug the two boys before he goes through the door. Last is Mr. Moreno, and then the policeman.

The door closes with a sigh and a hiss.

As soon as the door clicks the blonde woman walks away fast and the boys run ahead of her, the older boy chasing the younger one, and the friends who had been joking and laughing drift away slowly, and the woman in the car drives away fast, the dog peering at me from the back seat.

I walk up the street thinking of caged people and why we cage people and about the people who love the people who get caged every hour of every day in America, and then I walk past a slew of young oak trees all flittering and glowing in the late summer light, you know how in August the sunlight bends and everything seems lit up from the inside like you're in a movie?

# THE KNOCK

I met a guy who has two jobs in his town, policeman and soldier, and in both capacities he is the guy who knocks on doors to tell mothers and fathers and wives and husbands that their son or daughter or husband or wife is dead. He has to knock on a door five or six times a year, he says, and he has become a student of doors, and recently he talked about it.

First of all, he says, you never *ever* bang on the door, even if you are knocking for like the fifth time and you have been there freezing on the porch for ten minutes already. I always start with my knuckles and then go to the knocker or the bell if I have to. Most doors have a good loud hollow sound when you knock on them. Usually people answer right away. You would think that with houses bigger than they used to be that the people inside would be further away and wouldn't be able to hear a knock on the door but this isn't so. Women answering the door look first to see who you are whereas men just open it. I don't think I have ever had a child open the door. Only apartment and condo doors have chains, in my experience. I always wear one uniform or the other, depending on the circumstances. When I wear my military uniform the people know immediately why I am there, whereas if I am a policeman it could be anything. People ask me if I have found their lost dog or if there's a fire or if I am selling raffle tickets or whatever. I have had people cry in my arms, yes. Some people invite me in and give me tea even after I have delivered the news. It's like their automatic pilot function is courtesy, you know? I have had some people who refused to believe me, yes. And some who got angry and asked me to leave, yes. I have never had anyone swing at me, although I have heard stories like that. The thing I look for is shock. I have had people faint, men as well as women. People can go into serious shock and you have to be prepared for that. I carry a medical kit in the car. I rarely see children. I try to make visits in the late morning. Dogs are not usually a problem. I stay as long as necessary. Sometimes I have been in houses for hours. Sometimes I have waited with the person all afternoon until his or her spouse comes home from work. You mostly just listen. People tell stories. Often their first reaction, after the initial shock and grief, is to tell stories. People have to get their feelings out. I have heard thousands of stories. People tell me I should write them down but I feel that they are private stories, you know, stories that only came to me because someone's heart broke in the kitchen, and it wouldn't be right to make them public. I also bring information as regards counseling and funeral arrangements and legal matters. Generally people aren't ready to discuss such details. Mostly they are just stunned. They do want to discuss the facts of the death, yes. They want to know every last detail. It is a difficult job, yes, and it wears you down, but I try to do it with as much dignity and courtesy as possible. Yes, there are more military visits now with the recent wars, but I still make far more visits as a policeman. Probably the message I deliver most is that a loved one has been killed in an automobile accident. Often teenagers. The hardest messages to deliver are the deaths of children. There is nothing I can say to a mother or a father in that situation other than the facts of the matter. I have often thought that really what I am doing is a communal act, you know, like I am for a moment actually the town itself, standing there on the porch. I stand straight and speak clearly and wear the full uniform. I ask permission to enter the domicile but I don't sit down. It's easier to speak directly if you stand. I remove my hat and make sure the person is sitting down if possible and then deliver the message. I stay as long as it seems necessary. If I am absolutely sure the initial shock is lessened and the person is safe to be alone, I express my sorrow and condolences and prepare to leave.

At the door, before I put my hat on and go, I usually add that I will keep the deceased in my prayers. I make clear that I am saying this as a private citizen, not as soldier or policeman. In my experience saying that, about prayers, and meaning it, matters a lot to them. It matters to me also. That's about it. I'll check in on the person or family if necessary, and I keep abreast of funeral details and all, but I rarely go to the service, because I don't want to be a disruptive presence. I keep the deceased in my prayers for at least a month, longer if the deceased was a child. After a year or so I don't remember the adults, but I remember the children. I remember all the children. I wish I could forget their names but I can't. I could tell you every one. It would take quite a while. You have to be realistic, children get killed, they die in all sorts of ways, that's just what happens, but I remember them, yes. Someone has to.

# WHAT IT'S LIKE
# TO BE HIT BY A BULLET

Just for a moment this morning, between sips of coffee, before the dog wheedles a walk, let's poke through all the headlines about wars and shootouts and such, and let me tell you what it's like to be hit by a bullet.

We talk all the time about wars and conflicts and surges and police actions and international incursions and shootings and gunfire, but those are all just words for bullets hitting people, so this morning let's hear from a guy who got hit by a bullet.

My friend Donald is now a dignified silver-haired retired museum curator and former assistant principal who broke up race riots and had other interesting adventures like that during his career. In 1944 he was a skinny teenager fighting the Japanese all through the Pacific, mostly in New Guinea and the Philippines. He helped blow up Fort Drum in Manila Bay and was on Bataan, among other very difficult places to be.

Donald has many stories of hard and dark days and nights skippering his little two-man Army Boat Battalion landing craft — finding dead Japanese boy soldiers floating in the water, having a sniper shoot a huge coffee can under his arm ("boy, were we mad losing that coffee"), heading off on a raid and discovering the battalion drunk had drained the alcohol from every compass. But he told me a story the other day that says something simple and awful and powerful, and it was so blunt and direct about bullets that I think you should hear it too.

I was hit once by a bullet, he says, and when you get hit by a bullet you never ever forget what it feels like. It feels like you got hit with the biggest rock there ever was. We were going along in the boat and we went around a beach where there was a battle, and a slug hit me in the armpit and knocked me right over. The bullet was almost spent, it had travelled pretty far, but still it went into me a couple inches and it knocked me over like I was punched by Joe Louis. My buddy in the boat pulled the bullet out and poured sulfa in and the sulfa hurt worse than the bullet. Guys said later I should have put in for a Purple Heart but that'd be wrong.

Listen, you hear a lot of talk about so-and-so getting shot but I am here to tell you that getting shot even with a bullet that's mostly spent hurts like hell. I was terrified. I'll never forget the feeling. We use all these words for bullets hitting people but we don't know what the hell we are saying. We are saying that whoever got hit feels like he got hit with the biggest rock there ever was, and that he was terrified. Anyway we just kept going that day, after my buddy pulled the bullet out. Most of what wars are is you just keep going.

No, I didn't keep it. That kind of souvenir is for idiots and movies. I never got hit again, although the Japanese sure kept shooting at me. But I sure remember what it was like to get hit with a bullet. Sometimes I wish anyone who says anything whatsoever positive about war has to pay for his remark by getting hit with a bullet that's almost spent. He wouldn't get hurt real bad but he'd be sore for a week and he sure would be careful with words about wars ever after, you know what I'm saying?

# A NIGHT IN THE INFIRMARY

I bet nearly every student at every college in America spent a night in the college infirmary, at some shaky point of their undergraduating, and every boy or girl who did so probably shivered with the same fear and fascination and amazement that I did, partly because you were actually *in* the belly of the building we all passed a thousand times but never actually thought about, like you never actually thought about the football stadium or the laundry building unless you were assigned there somehow. Maybe you had to spend a night in the infirmary under observation because the nurse thought probably you had a concussion, although it was hard, she said, to find a concussion under all that hair, which made me a laugh, a little, but it hurt to laugh, so she fell silent and took my temperature again.

Where are you from, son?

New York City.

So you have had plenty of concussions, eh?

I remember long narrow hallways with mullioned windows, and polite professional people who murmured gently, and I remember that it was cold, and that the sheets in the bed were beautifully starched, as if an army of grandmothers laboring in the basement were producing crackling redolent bedclothes so wonderfully clean and pressed that it seemed a shame to fold back the covers and infest them with my adolescent self, but I did so, because the nurse told me to, and she was terse and sturdy, and I was in her spotless bailiwick, not in the shaggy chaos of my usual life in the residence halls. This was no dorm, despite the familiar turtle-green paint and the ancient iron beds; this was the island of the ill, where voices were soft and machinery hummed, where the few other students I saw were curled and pale in their beds, under the old hairy blankets the university must have bought by the thousands from the government, perhaps just after the Peloponnesian War.

Can you hear me, son?

Yes, ma'am.

We've decided not to replace your brain with an apple, alright?

Yes, ma'am.

My concussion, under all that hair, had been incurred when I landed head-first on the basketball floor of the vast student rec center, after soaring in admirable fashion to try to block a shot above the rim but tripping on a guy and somersaulting and ending up imprinting my face in the rubber, a weird image that may still be there like the haunted visage on the Shroud of Turin, although that gaunt Jewish guy looked cooler than me. I looked like a dissolute John Lennon then.

You're a sophomore, son?

Yes, ma'am.

So you have roommates.

Yes.

But they are sophomores also.

Yes.

So none of you can be trusted with hourly overnight observation.

No, ma'am.

So I spent the night in the infirmary. I seemed to be partly blind, and had a roaring headache, and was Officially Damaged, there was a Chart, there was a Consulting Physician, there would be sheaves of reports, my parents would be notified, and already they had received pink slips indicating Academic Difficulty, which caused my father's face to tighten and my mother's smile to fade, and I had finally arrived at an age when I first noticed threads of sadness in their faces and began to have a dim appreciation of how hard they had worked for their rude and selfish children, how much they had sacrificed, how much I had hurt them with sneer and snide, how much they loved me and could not say, for all their articulate wit and professional eloquence as journalist and teacher; and here I was, yet again, a cause of pain for them.

I'll wake you every hour to check your eyes.

Yes, ma'am.

Are you scared?

Yes, ma'am.

I'll send someone.

She sent another nurse. I don't remember her name. I don't remember the color of her uniform, her eyes or her stature or her age or anything else except her voice and her hands, which were cool and warm at the same time. I remember that she spoke quietly, and that whatever it was that she said calmed me and helped me sleep, and I remember that she was there again and again that night, perhaps all night long.

In the morning I was released from the infirmary with instructions to lay low and have a roommate wake me every hour the next night, which my roommate did with his usual high glee, since he was the most cheerful boy in the history of the galaxy and had been a wrestling champion famous for laughing during matches, which infuriated his opponents, which may have led to their defeat, which would not be the first time joy outwitted rage.

I called my parents that day and admitted I loved them and apologized for having been such a selfish ass. My mother was delighted. My father, a wise man, wondered why I was really calling. I did not see those nurses again, but I didn't forget them, and something about their quiet humor and intent grace was a seed in me as far as savoring the grace of people who serve other people, especially lanky children secretly desperate to find out who they are and what they will do with their wild and lovely lives, which is the definition of Undergraduate. My mother, now 89 years old, dearly loves to tell people that her middle son, at the ripe old age of nineteen, awoke from many years of pure and unadulterated selfishness and telephoned to say he was sorry. *I remember it was October,* says my mom, with dark pleasure. *I believe it was October nineteenth, in fact. Let me check with your father.* I would sigh at the high glee with which my mom likes to tell this story, but I know very well that maybe the moment I stopped thinking only of myself was the moment college mattered the most to me. I've been going to college ever since.

# HOMEWORK PROBLEMS

Q: If a man is walking south along a beach at one mile an hour, and a woman a mile behind him is walking south along the same beach at two miles an hour, at what point will they just totally misunderstand each other and fail to communicate in even the simplest and most basic ways about anything and everything including sex, money, disciplining the children, where to vacation, and the whole tiresome argument about whether the dish rack should be wood or steel?

----

A falcon flying at fifty miles an hour spots a duck flying at thirty miles an hour and a pigeon flying at twenty miles an hour, in that clunky flaring weird-bird way that pigeons fly, you know how they careen through the air sometimes like someone hit them with a broomstick? You know what I mean? Q: Why do they do that funky shaking-their-groove-thang walk anyway? Is it a put-on? Are they just totally goofing on human beings or what?

----

Q: If a deer and an elk mate, whose insurance plan covers the children? And is their union legal in Massachusetts?

----

A train going seven hundred miles an hour encounters a vole. Q: Why exactly is the train going that fast? Does being in such a hurry mean that you are important? Or is being in such a hurry a secret sign of terrible insecurity, a quivering fear of being alone with one's inner train-ness?

You are playing golf, and your partner lashes a terrific eight-iron shot from about a hundred yards out, in mucky conditions, the shot of her life, and her ball *juuust* catches the fringe above the hole, and what appears to be a gust of wind nudges it *juuust* at the crucial second, and the ball heads straight for the hole, and is at most, like, ten inches away, on a true line, as far as you can tell, but suddenly o my god a *heron* lands on the green! and *eats* the ball! which it cannot properly digest! and the bird keels over dead as a door right there on the green! Q: Do you concede the putt?

A bobcat, a cougar, and a house cat that denies ever knowingly accepting steroids from Balco Laboratories in California have a fight. Q: Should the event be pay-per-view or regular cable?

A poet gives a reading of his new experimental work, which surges past the cultural need for narrative or indeed form of any kind whatsoever and approaches, as he says eloquently in his prefatory remarks, *pure* poetry, which does not need words, nor music, nor the usual culturally fascist insistence on sense or story. Q: How long should he be sentenced to community service cleaning public toilets?

Three novelists eat a vast and sumptuous dinner, complete with several bottles of terrific wine and more oysters than you can shimmy your jimmy at. The waiter, with some trepidation, brings the bill. Q: How many hours do the novelists wait at their table for an editor to happen by?

---

You are fishing a tiny stream in Oregon. Many years ago this stream, during the fabulous salmon runs of yore, was crammed with so many salmon returning to spawn that a man could haul a small piano out onto their backs and run through the collected works of Liberace without ever getting his feet wet. However, what with pollution and logging runoff and overfishing and all that Liberace, no wild salmon in thirty years has run up your stream...until today! You hook the amazing creature, and wrassle it to shore, and face a moral dilemma. Q: White wine or red?

---

A boy goes to the store and buys ten apples for five cents, five oranges for three cents, and nineteen pears for two cents. Q: What planet are you on to get such prices? And who gave the kid the dime? Is that the dime I left right here on this table not five minutes ago? How many times have I told you that every penny counts in this family, not to mention dimes? Do you want to eat nothing but air for the next eight years? What exactly am I going to do with nineteen pears? Do you want salmon with pear sauce? Should we invite the novelists?

# YOUR FINAL EXAM

Consider a particle emission from a $^{238}$U nucleus. The nucleus emits the particle with energy $E_\alpha = 4.2 \times 10^6$ eV. If the particle is contained inside the nuclear radius of $r_N \approx 7 \times 10^{-15}$ m, what is the distance that the particle travels through the barrier?

Well, duh. The distance is about as far as a sneeze travels if you really let that sucker go and get your whole body into it, or the distance between the moment when you realize you have to pee like a racehorse and the actual highway exit finally appears, or the distance between a guy and his girlfriend after he says he has a little amusing ha ha crush on her sister ha ha isn't that funny?

Talk about traveling through the barrier.

Or the distance between age eight, when you thought you were going to be an astronaut or a fireman or a pro surfer or maybe all three at once, scheduling rocket launches in winter and surfing in summer and firefighting in between, moments when the cool bell rang in your cool house in which there would be a cool pole just like in the firehouse so you could jump out of bed and slide down the pole right into your cool car, and middle age, when recently you were talking learnedly about *assessed value*.

Or the distance between the words *I* and *do* on your wedding day.

Or the distance between the stunned silent joy in your head after your daughter slid out of your wife and the horrendous shriek you heard this morning when with all the good intentions in the world you opened the bathroom door to give her a towel *like she asked you to for heaven's sake.*

Or the distance between the great idea of civic responsibility and the guy standing in the rain outside the jail door late in the afternoon with all his personal effects in a plastic grocery bag and his kids staring at him from the back seat of the ratty car across the street where the woman driving refuses to look at him.

Or the distance between the great idea of the international right of self-determination and a Private First Class age nineteen pointing his rifle at a kid age seven on the chance that the kid might have an Improvised Explosive Device strapped around his Thin Scrawny Chest.

Or the distance between might and right.

Or the distance between must and just.

Or the distance between the dad you thought you were going to be and the kind of dad you actually are.

Or the distance between act and apology.

Or the distance between making a boatload of money and making your money fix a lot of leaky boats.

Or the distance between your house and the emergency room when your kid is bleeding all over the car and even though you know it's just a sliced ear and there's no way he's going to die or lose the floppy thing still the way he sobs makes you absolutely roaring blind with gibbering fear.

Or the distance between an elderly lady's lips and the rising flood waters in New Orleans as she sits in her wheelchair in her living room with the water at her neck and as she said later *honey I prayed like I never prayed before.*

Or the distance between people who used to be married to each other.

Or the distance between your lips and the lips of the first girl you ever kissed in the paneled basement of her friend's house in the dark as you lean in and she leans in and neither of you knows what's supposed to happen or why or how.

Or the distance between the falling falcon and the yearning earth.

Or the length in millimeters of the umbilical cord.

Or the distance between ideas and the ragged words we drape on them.

Or between possibility and probability.

Or poetry and prayer.

Or who we are,

And who we might still be.

# A NOTE ON POWER

As a skinny guy only seventy inches tall I was never much of a horse physically but I did have enough pop to beat up my kid brothers, which I did until *they* got powerful and I went off to college juuuuust in time. In college I kept thinking that power had to do with bodies, and that girls were impressed with muscles, and that burliness led to success, and it took forever for me to realize that this was a lie, that the word *musclehead* was no joke, and that women were really after hearts they could trust. Plus I started noticing that often the men and women who were most influential, most interesting, most startling, most amazing – most powerful, really – were, by pretty much every definition of powerful, powerless. They were skinny penniless guys like Christ and Gandhi, or cheerful brilliant cripples like Franklin Roosevelt and Flannery O'Connor, or stubborn dignified ladies like Rosa Parks and Ursula Le Guin, or unknown geeky guys with courage coming out of their ears like the guy who was carrying his grocery bags home one June day in Beijing in 1989 and suddenly had just about *enough* of army tanks rolling by to smash kids in Tiananmen Square and jumped into the street and made eighteen tanks stop and changed the world, didn't he? And isn't it cool, almost twenty years later, that no one knows who he is? And isn't what he did powerful beyond any words I can find to describe his courage? And aren't there a million acts of incredible power and poetry like that every day? Like the firemen who ran up inside the World Trade Center towers instead of running down as by all sense and reason and logic they should have? And the millions of mothers who move recalcitrant heaven and sweet bruised earth daily to find enough bread and water for their magic holy babies? And the teenage boys who patrol, terrified but intent, through the murk and blood of Baghdad and Kabul for us? And the million business owners who scratch and kick and wrestle to stay in business because they know that if their companies fail whole families and clans and towns will sufferand are enraged at devious shifty corporate crime because it steals trust, the most crucial social coin of all?

I think about power all the time as a dad, too. In the old days, when my children were tiny and squirming and peeing on the floor like puppies, I was king, I made the rules, I fed and wiped and bathed, I thundered, I was the last word. (Well, the second-to-last word; as my daughter noted wryly when quite small, "Mom is the boss and you are the second boss.") But now that hormone hurricanes have swept through the house and my kids are suddenly supercilious teenagers, I have only the power to persuade, to suggest, to remonstrate, to hint, to remind, to confound, to complicate their brilliant and confused hearts. It took me a while to shift gears from boss to bemused, but I might suggest that we are all in the same boat, and whenever you think you are powerful you are pretty much not; or, in other words, what makes you powerful – money or position or brains – is only useful if you use it to elevate other people. Power is a cool tool, but tools at rest are only sculptures, lovely and useless.

Listen, I know what you are thinking: what does all this have to do with me and my business and my career? And I reply: I am only reminding you of what you already know in your heart. You spent years finding and focusing your skills and talents and gifts and ideas and creativity and energies, and now you have a career, you're supporting a family, you employ a lot of people maybe, you give away gobs of cash for good causes, but sometimes deep down at night you wonder if there's *some* way to do more to really change things, you know? To really hammer hunger and poverty and the shiver of fear that haunts families without insurance or next month's rent or much more in the pantry than pasta, to stitch a world where your kids won't be afraid of murderers in Afghani caves or fouled water or joblessness?

Man, I wonder that too, all the time, late at night, and I wrack my scrap of brains, and I conclude that for me it's stories; my job is to collect and tell stories and try to connect people along electric holy lines, but what is it for you? How can you bend your startling tools in new ways? How can the most creative and inventive and energetic and powerful men and women in America – that's *you* – lead us past political patter and preacher-prattle?

I don't know much, but I know this: this country, for all its muddle and wrangle, is the most extraordinary national idea that ever was, and it's still possible that America will lead the way past mere power to a planetary peace that surpasseth understanding. No politician or poet will lead us there. It will be someone like you, yes *you*, you reading this in bed or at the kitchen table or in the car while waiting for a dad or daughter, you who creates ideas, who articulates and defends and shares them in the public market, who mills ideas into food and education and healing for thousands of people, who understands that power only matters, finally, when it is a verb. You who know full well, in the bone of your soul, that power that doesn't work for the powerless is only flash and glitter, vanity and chaff, a hall of mirrors for staring endlessly and uselessly at yourself; which is a good definition of hell.

# WHAT IF?

Some time ago I was in a pub in Australia when two cheerful men stopped by my table. They were older, friendly, both professors, and both, it turned out, professional philosophers in Melbourne. We got to talking. We got into a great wild conversation about how thoughts are actually electrical explosions in the wet living mud of the brain, and how genetics is actually a form of mathematics if you think about it, and how religions are biological constructs at base, being formed by the innate human urge to gather into clans and tribes and teams and being informed by the innate human urge for awe and respect and prayer, but right there our opinions diverged like the Yarra and the Don and the Dee, for they believed that religions were only evolutionary urges at heart, whereas I believe religions are, for all their proven blood and greed, still hints and intimations, lodestars and compass points, possibilities and verbs hurrying us home to the sea of mercy.

The philosophers were brilliant men, waaay more learned than me, and they flopped dark history on the table between us like an ugly shark. Words like knives: Inquisition, Shoah, Troubles.

And yet and yet, gentlemen, I said, are there not also stunning prophets and visionaries, Maimonides and Mertons, Tutus and Tukurams, grinning brave Dalai Lamas, tough little relentless Teresas of Calcutta? Does not Islam, for all the seething madness of the modern murderer cowering in a cave, say that forgiveness is justice? Did not Gandhi forgive his assassin with his last breath? Did not a pope recently kneel and apologize? Are there not more than two hundred references to the holiness of forgiveness in the Qur'an? Did not the Prophet himself ask for forgiveness and sing the endless mercy of the One, a song maybe bloodthirsty bin Laden ought to have learned the words to? Is not the point of all religion to push us past our easy violence into some new country?

They smiled, they demurred, for them religions were merely corrals, gathering points, reflections of the urge to crowd together against predators, organize into teams for efficient collection of food, bind together in clusters for warmth. Religions, said one of the philosophers, are finally no different than footy teams and nations and sewing clubs; we are made to collect in clans, and will do so on any excuse, which explains heavy metal concerts and Star Trek conventions, for example.

We laughed and soon parted, the philosophers back to parsing Kierkegaard or pondering neutrinos or whatever and me eventually back to my own country, but I have continued to think about that conversation, almost every day, because I still have faith in faith, despite all the evidence that the philosophers are right and religions are merely nutty hobbies, like being a Cubs fan. I keep thinking that under the rituals and rigmarole of religion there is a crucial wriggling possibility for what human beings might someday be. It's the same possibility you see sometimes, for an instant, under patriotism or sport or families: a humor and mercy, a camaraderie and ease, a grace and mercy, a warmth beyond all reason and sense. Sometimes, for a second, at a game, a meeting, in line at the bank, during a wedding receptionor a park by the river, you get a flash of connective energy with your fellow beings – just a flick of it, a hint, a glance, a quick shiver of inexplicable peace and joy in the company of your fellow travelers.

That flash is what all religions are for. Yes, we gather because deep in our mammal hearts we are in awe of whatever it is that sparks life, and yes, we are desperate for definition so we drape explanations on the Unnameable, and yes, we gather in groups because we must, because we are mammals just down from the trees, as the great American sage Peter Matthiessen says, and we are afraid of death, which is why we deliver it to others so easily. But *what if*, as Peter also says? What if our moral evolution ever caught up to our breathtaking physical evolution? *What if?*

We can move mountains and fly to the moon, we can murder by the millions and map the mystery of our genetic making, but what if we ever dropped the dagger, plucked the beams from our eyes, and grew up? *What if?* And we have maps of that bright country already, in the brilliant bones of every religion. There are and have been many thousands of religions, each stridently different, all flawed and greedy, but all, in their absolute essence, about the same thing: praise for the miracle of life, awe for the mysterious force that creates life, yearning for life beyond death, and, most of all, inarticulate desperation for a future in which mercy trumps murder. More than any other force on this bruised earth, religions keep that desperate dream alive; for which this morning I sing and celebrate them, and bow to what is best in us. What if...?

# WHAT AM I DOING HERE?

Dishes, mostly. And gobs of laundry. You wouldn't think three kids would have so much laundry, I mean how many shirts can three kids possibly *wear*, it's not like we live in the Arctic and they have to have twenty layers of fabric so they can go trap wolverine for pin money or whatever, but you don't know *these* kids, these are their *mother's* kids, and thus genetically far more attentive to graceful appearance than their dad, who looks like a dissolute wolverine. *These* kids are apparently ornate musical productions with lots of costume changes, and the way they clean their rooms on Saturdays is to shovel all the clothes on the floor down the laundry chute at the bottom of which is their father, roaring.

But I asked for these children, I begged for them, I prayed and yearned and was thrilled and delighted when they emerged from my wife one after another like a circus act, and I wrote lyrical sentimental muck about them when they were little, and now that they are lanky and sneering in ways I could never have imagined, I cannot retract the vows and oaths I swore when they were born, which were that I would expend every ounce of energy and creativity to be their most excellent and attentive dad, which I have tried to be for fifteen years, with middling success and a stunning amount of laundry and roaring. I got exactly what I asked the Coherent Mercy for, which was the chaos and hubbub of children, who are the most extraordinary creatures of all, and I have often thought that what I am here for, if I can get over the whole laundry problem for a minute, is them. Also I have often thought that the Coherent Mercy has a dark and devious sense of humor, and clearly relishes irony, and often gives you exactly what you asked for, which is more than you knew you wanted.

Also I am here for sunlight and hawks and the way dragonflies and damselflies do that geometric astounding zigzag thing in the air totally effortlessly which absolutely knocks me out and I have spent many hours staring at them in a trance, explaining to people that I am conducting a scientific project. They look at me oddly. And I am here to hear thrushes in late winter and to gape at osprey and to taste my way judiciously through excellent red wines from countries where the sun shines. And to shuffle humming through the rain, gentle and ancient and patient and persistent and holier than we ever admit. And to hear and foment laughter, the coolest sound there is. And to witness grace under duress; that more than anything.

———

I have often thought that I am the luckiest guy on earth, for any number of reasons, starting with being born American of Irish ancestry in New York, what a combination of swaggering cultural confidence and addiction to tall tales and the music of stories and the insistence that creative energy can jolt the universe, and then I was a middle child, balanced between the weight of expectation and too much independence, and I was a child of the middle class and so was fed and clothed and safe and educated and no one shot at me, and in college I woke up a little spiritually and mentally and socially, and then I shuffled on into a life utterly absorbed by stories, their swing and cadence and bone and song, and a cool woman married me and I have had a sweet confusing painful delighted mysterious marriage that is different every eleven minutes, which is riveting and frustrating and riveting, and we were graced with all these children, some of them twins who move so fast I am never quite sure how many twins there are in the house at all one bit, and I lucked into work that has everything to do with listening and hearing stories and catching stories and shaping stories and sharing stories, and at age fifty I conclude that I was born and made for stories. I am a storyman,

I believe with all my hoary heart that stories save lives, and the telling and hearing of them is a holy thing, powerful far beyond our ken, sacramental, crucial, nutritious; without the sea of stories in which we swim we would wither and die; we are here for each other, to touch and be touched, to lose our tempers and beg forgiveness, to listen and to tell, to hail and farewell, to laugh and to snarl, to use words as knives and caresses, to puncture lies and to heal what is broken.

———

There are two words in the lore of Judaism, our parent stock, the branch of the human family that heard the words *I Am Who Am* (the bluntest syntax in the history of the world!), and these two words, tikkun olam, תִּיקּוּן עוֹלָם in the Hebrew, are easy to translate but hard to explain. My friends who speak the ancient tongue tell me the words mean repairing the world, that the universe when it was imagined into being could not hold the unimaginable infinity of the Word, and so it shattered into countless shards and shreds, and our job, the job of every human being, perhaps every living being of every shape and size, is, by living intently and attentively, by being our truest and greatest selves, to work to repair and restore the broken gift. I think this is true, and by now, after fifty years, I am absolutely sure what I am supposed to do: sense stories, catch some by their brilliant tails as they rocket by, carve and sculpt them into arrows, and fire them into the hearts of as many people as I can reach on this bruised and blessed planet. That's all. That's enough.

———

A few days after the murders of September 11 a magazine editor called me and asked if I would contribute an essay to a special issue she and her colleagues were hurriedly making in the aftermath of September 11. Nope, I said. Three of my friends were roasted to white ash that day by that foul coward Bin Laden, and his crimes had already produced an ocean of empty opinion and windy rhetoric and witless commentary around the world, and the easy fatuous opinions enraged me, everyone so confident they knew what to say in the face of the unspeakable, and I refused to add to the babble, and would try to offer the only eloquent and apt thing that could or should be said in the aftermath of such horror, which is nothing. The only proper thing in your mouth at such a time is prayer, best said silently.

In the kitchen that night I reported this conversation to my wife and daughter.

So what are you going to do? asked my daughter.

Pray.

But what are you going to *do*?

What do you mean?

Well, Dad, you are always lecturing us about how if God gives you a talent and you don't use that talent that's a sin, and, you know, no offense, Dad, but you only have the one talent, you say so yourself, and that's telling stories, so if you don't tell a story here, isn't that a sin? No offense.

In the next three months I wrote three stories, one for each of my friends, Tommy Crotty and Farrell Lynch and Sean Lynch, whose wives sleep alone and whose children are unfathered, and published them in magazines, and gave them to anthologies, and badgered newspapers and newsletters and parish bulletins and editors in other countries to reprint them for free, and copied and mailed them to as many people as I could think of, and put them in a book of essays, and I still don't think I did enough to mill my small peculiar gift into an arrow of furious hope against the dark arrogance of Osama Bin Laden, who was sure he knew the mind of God and like every twisted soul who murders under the banner of heaven is destined to hear the sobs of children until the end of time. I spent years plotting ways to rain stories down on Bin Laden in his cave and eventually flush him out into the angry light, harried by stories like vengeful hawks; then a bullet found him first in his sprawling suburban mansion. There was a shard of holiness in that man, somewhere, down below the twisted ego and squirming rage; he was a holy child once, a long time ago; I hope the Lord forgives him.

When I was a kid I wanted in the worst way to be a pro basketball player, though even I had to admit that there didn't seem to be a whole lot of job opportunities for short skinny guys with ponytails and thick glasses. When I got older all I really wanted was to be loved by and to be in love with a fascinating woman. It took me a long time to realize that all women are fascinating and that being in love with and being loved by one was a wondrous gift but not a destination, a verb and not a noun; in fact I learned that being married to one was only a much deeper form of excitement and confusion than the series of muddled love affairs we engage in before we marry. Not until a few years ago did I realize that I was on earth not to be loved but to love. That's all. That's enough.

I am here to witness. I was sent to sing. I am here to catch and tell the story of the teacher who ran with a child on her shoulders out of the ash and fire of September 11. I am here to tell you that a man and a woman reached for each other at the high windows in the south tower and they held hands as they leapt into the void. I am here to tell you that a man carried a colleague eighty floors to the street and then went back in. I am here to marvel at a pope praying with his almost-assassin, to marvel at victims forgiving the murderers of their children in South Africa, to be riveted by all the thin bony nuns who have carried the church on their shoulders for centuries and hardly anyone ever shouted *my god without those women there would be no church whatever whatsoever absolutely!* I am here to hear all the stories of all the women who have bent every ounce and iota of their souls to love, which is pretty much all the women who ever lived. I am here to see unreasonable illogical nonsensical courage and faith. I am here to sing grace under duress. I am a storycatcher, charged with finding stories that matter, stories about who we are at our best, who we might be still, because without stories we are only mammals with weapons. I am here to point at shards of holiness. That's all. That's enough.

# PROVENANCE

"A Sin," "The Senator," "All Legs & Curiosity," "The You of You," "One Night," "Your Final Exam," "Advice to My Son," "Homework Problems," and a version of "The Genius of American Catholicism" all appeared in the University of Portland's wonderfully odd and ambitious *Portland Magazine* – see www.up.edu/portlandmag.

"Journal: Ash Street," appeared in *Portland Monthly* magazine in Oregon, thanks to Ted Katauskas and Camela Raymond.

"[Silence]," "The Next Eleven," "Mute Riven Blessed," "The Terrible Brilliance," "Litany of the Blessed Mother," "Let It Go," and "His Father" appeared in *U.S. Catholic* magazine, published in Chicago by the Claretians; particular thanks to cheerful editor Cathy O'Connell-Cahill.

"Pong Ping" appeared in *The Melbourne Anglican*, in Melbourne, Australia, thanks to oenophile Roland Ashby, and then in *Blue Mesa Review*, courtesy of Nari Kirk.

"The Word" appeared in *Notre Dame Business* magazine, thanks to editor Mary Hamman and publisher Carolyn Woo.

"A Note on Pornography" appeared in *The Catholic Sentinel* newspaper in Portland, Oregon, thanks to Ed Langlois and the brilliant enigma Robert Pfohman.

"Irreconcilable Dissonance," "Cool Things," and "A Note on Secrets" appeared in *Oregon Humanities* magazine, published in Portland by the Oregon Council for the Humanities, thanks to editor Kathleen Holt.

"The Order in Which People are Admitted to Heaven" and "What Am I Doing Here?" appeared in *Notre Dame Magazine*, thanks to editor Kerry Temple.

"Their Thin Bony Shoulders," "Rec League," "On Miraculousness," "Going to Jail" and "What It's Like to be Hit by a Bullet" appeared in *Eureka Street* webzine in Australia, thanks to Tim Kroenert. See www.erurekastreet.com.au.

"The Knock" appeared in *Commonweal* magazine, thanks to editor Patrick Jordan.

"A Night in the Infirmary" appeared in *North Dakota State University Magazine*, thanks to editor Laura McDaniel.

"A Note on Power" appeared in *Oregon Business* magazine, thanks to editor Robin Droussard.

"What If?" appeared in *The Age* newspaper in Australia, thanks to editor Sally Heath.

"A Child is Not a Furniture" appeared in the great webzine *Brevity*, thanks to editor Dinty Moore.

"Why Do We Say One Thing About Children But Do Another?" appeared in *The Oregonian* newspaper in Portland, thanks to editor Peggy McMullen.

# Also by Brian Doyle